A Walk Through Paris

A Walk Through Paris

Eric Hazan

Translated by David Fernbach

VERSO
London • New York

This English-language edition published by Verso 2018
Originally published in French as *Une traversée de Paris*
© Éditions du Seuil 2016
Translation © David Fernbach 2018

This book is supported by the Institut français (Royamme-
Uni) as part of the Burgess programme.

1 3 5 7 9 10 8 6 4 2

Verso
UK: 6 Meard Street, London W1F 0EG
US: 20 Jay Street, Suite 1010, Brooklyn, NY 11201
versobooks.com

Verso is the imprint of New Left Books

ISBN-13: 978-1-78663-258-6
ISBN-13: 978-1-78663-260-9 (UK EBK)
ISBN-13: 978-1-78663-261-6 (US EBK)

British Library Cataloguing in Publication Data
A catalogue record for this book is available from the British Library

Library of Congress Cataloging-in-Publication Data
A catalog record for this book is available from the Library of Congress

Library of Congress Cataloging-in-Publication Data

Names: Hazan, Eric, author.
Title: A walk through Paris / Eric Hazan.
Other titles: Traversée de Paris. French
Description: Brooklyn, New York : Verso, 2018. |
Identifiers: LCCN 2017048932 (print) | LCCN 2017052776 (ebook) | ISBN
   9781786632609 () | ISBN 9781786632616 () | ISBN 9781786632586
   (hardback)
Subjects: LCSH: Paris (France)—Description and travel. | Paris
   (France)—History. | Hazan, Eric—Homes and haunts—France—Paris. |
   Publishers and publishing—France—Biography. |
   Surgeons—France—Biography. | Historians—France—Biography. | BISAC:
   TRAVEL / Europe / France. | SOCIAL SCIENCE / Sociology / Urban. |
HISTORY
   / Europe / France.
Classification: LCC DC707 (ebook) | LCC DC707 .H43713 2018 (print) | DDC
   914.4/361048412—dc23
LC record available at https://lccn.loc.gov/2017048932

Typeset in Sabon by MJ&N Gavan, Truro, Cornwall
Printed and bound by CPI Group (UK) Ltd, Croydon, CR0 4YY

For Cléo

Contents

Acknowledgements   ix

1. From the centre of Ivry to the 'Barrière d'Italie',
   via the Porte d'Ivry and the Avenue de Choisy   1
2. From the Place d'Italie to the 85 bus terminus
   via the Place Denfert-Rochereau   15
3. From the Luxembourg garden to Les Halles
   via the Pont-Neuf   49
4. From Châtelet to Beaubourg via the battlefield
   of Saint-Méry   75
5. From the Rue Quincampoix to the Strasbourg-
   Saint-Denis crossroads via the Rue Saint-Denis   91
6. From the Porte Saint-Denis to the Place de la
   Chapelle via the Faubourg Saint-Denis and the
   Gare du Nord   115
7. From La Chapelle-Saint-Denis to the Porte de
   la Chapelle via three different itineraries: the
   Rue Marx-Dormoy/Rue de la Chapelle axis, La
   Goutte-d'Or, Rue Pajol and Rue de l'Évangile   139
8. From the Boulevard Ney to Saint-Denis along
   the A1 autoroute   165

Notes   179
Index   185

Acknowledgements

Valérie Kubiak and Arrigo Lessana gave this manuscript a critical reading that helped a great deal towards its present form. Françoise Fromonot replied very willingly to my questions about contemporary architecture. Thomas Bouchet, François Chaslin and Jean-François Cabestan contributed valuable clarifications. To everyone who encouraged me on this walk, fraternal thanks.

CHAPTER I

In *The Trip Across Paris*, a film by Claude Autant-Lara from 1956, Jean Gabin and Bourvil walk through the night of the Occupation, made darker than usual by air-raid precautions that have put out the street lamps and covered the windows with blackout paper. The two rogues, carrying heavy suitcases filled with pork, proceed from the Rue Poliveau to the Rue Lepic – from the Jardin des Plantes to Montmartre. This was a very famous film in my youth, and even today Gabin's 'Poor bastards!' has the ring of a popular phrase. The story may well have inspired my title for this book, and perhaps the entire project, even if it has nothing in common with the adventures of Gabin and Bourvil, in which encounters with policemen in cycle capes, black-market traffickers, German patrols and ladies of the night, all to the sound of sirens, are comic episodes whose backdrops make Paris the setting of a night-time dream.

My own path is rather a daytime one, with a different orientation: from Ivry to Saint-Denis, more or less following the dividing line between the east and west of Paris, or what you could call the Paris meridian. I chose this itinerary without much consideration, but later on it became clear to me that it was no accident, that this line followed the meanders of an existence begun close to the Luxembourg garden, led for a long time opposite the Observatoire, and continued further to the east, in Belleville, at the time I am writing, but with long spells in the meantime in Barbès and on the north side of the Montmartre hill. And in fact, under the effect of the peerless mental exercise that is walking, memories have risen to the surface street by street, even very distant fragments of the past on the border of forgetfulness.

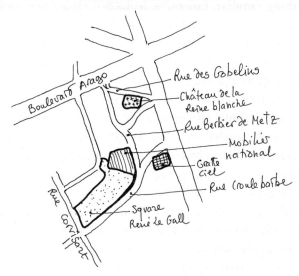

If this journey begins at Ivry it is because of a bookstore. Envie de Lire is not simply a shop that sells books, it is also a place of browsing and discovery. The piles of books, often unstable, are not arranged by chance, but linked by a thread that takes a moment to discern. Perhaps you won't find the title you've come to look for, but no matter, you will leave carrying a book of photography or philosophy, a Mexican novel or the memoirs of a forgotten revolutionary. These small premises on the Rue Gabriel-Péri are propitious for discussion, even argument. Readings from new books finish late, and groups on the pavement are in no hurry to disperse as the staff finally bring in the boxes of books open to all under the arcade. The business is a cooperative, so does not have an owner; but R., solidly built as Spaniards can be, is both the soul of the place and the representative of an endangered species, that of poetic communists.

Another reason for choosing Ivry as my starting point is its remarkable town centre, in which Envie de Lire is a lively presence. This is an architectural ensemble unlike anything familiar. Emerging from the Métro and looking upward, you are struck by a tangle of points, sharp corners, irregular polygons, gangways and planted terraces, all in raw concrete. Small apartment blocks, all designed to be slightly different, are linked by direct contact or by a network of stairways and overhead passages, creating a three-dimensional labyrinth. Enclosed in the general tangle, half a dozen small towers punctuate a landscape whose grey concrete is softened by the overflowing green of the planted terraces.

The architects, Renée Gailhoustet and Jean Renaudie, took thirty years to build this ensemble, from the early 1960s to the late 1980s, at a time when, in the name of town-planning, the banlieue was falling victim both to 'zoning' – different activities pigeonholed into distinct zones – and to high-rise blocks and concrete slabs. Their aim, on the contrary, was to superimpose functions, mixing together shops, services, artists' studios, crèches, schools, offices and housing, in an attempt at collective living made possible by the support of the communist municipality. Renée Gailhoustet herself lives in the quarter that she built. From her terrace planted with fruit trees, she shows me how, by way of these staggered spaces, superimposed and almost attached, connections are established between the tenants. She tells me how she designed the tower apartments to create duplexes with two aspects, and all the tricks she came up with to make this social housing as pleasant as that of the rich.

The exit from the Mairie-d'Ivry station opens onto a noisy avenue widened into a square. This does not continue eastward, towards the Paris cemetery and Villejuif, being blocked by a hill with a small medieval church on its summit and, behind it, a rural cemetery just a hundred metres from the flow of cars. Traffic is routed towards Paris on a road that bears the name of Ivry's great man, Maurice Thorez. This is bordered with shacks, workshops, garages, small factories, low-rise apartment blocks – a landscape you cross without really looking at it, though not lacking in charm. From time to time, you have a view of lower Ivry and the Seine, marked out by the smoke from urban chimneys and the concrete spire indicating the red high-rise of the Cité Maurice-Thorez.

My view of Thorez is mixed. A docile executor of Stalin's policy, champion of productivism in the wake of Liberation, organizer of Moscow trials in Paris, and a thoroughly detestable character. But despite everything, despite himself, his name remains bound to the memory of a time when, for masses of young people of whom I was one, communism had nothing to do with the terrible system that repressed Eastern Europe. It was a world in which fraternal relations were forged by way of meetings, demonstrations, actions conducted joyfully in common, not to mention holidays. I owe a great debt to my communist comrades at the Lycée

Ivry, Avenue Maurice-Thorez.

Louis-le-Grand and then the PCB (physics, chemistry, biology) preparatory year for medical studies, held in a brick building opposite the entrance to the Jardin des Plantes alongside Cuvier's house. It was due to them that I broke with the world for which, as the son of a good bourgeois family of assimilated Jews, everything marked me out – broke definitively, even if the professions I went on to practise, surgery and publishing, do not count among the most proletarian. Despite the likes of Garaudy, Kanapa and Thorez, I do not believe it right to treat everything concerning the communism of those years as 'Stalinist', nor to deny my own part in this. If truth be told, I am even rather proud of it.

At the Porte d'Ivry as elsewhere, the meeting point between banlieue and city is neither gentle nor pleasant. In 1860, when Paris annexed the immediately surrounding communes to complete its twenty arrondissements, the connection was formed quite naturally. Passing today from the Rue du Faubourg-du-Temple to the Rue de Belleville, you do not have the impression of crossing an obstacle, despite passing the site of a former city gate, the Belleville *barrière* in the Wall of the Farmers-General. Sometimes the transition is a little more awkward, as between the Rue du Faubourg-Poissonnière and the Rue des Poissonniers across the complicated Barbès intersection, or between the Avenue des Gobelins and the Avenue d'Italie across the Place d'Italie, but there is no real problem here.

Between the city of Paris and the outlying communes, however, things are quite different, particularly to the north and east, where crossing from Paris to the banlieue on foot may be quite an adventure. At the Porte des Lilas, despite the Périphérique being underground, you have to cross a great void between the last social housing blocks of the Boulevard Mortier and the first old houses of the Rue de

Paris in Les Lilas, with a tiny green space to the left (the Serge-Gainsbourg garden which, according to a notice, is an example of 'urban continuity' – a fine denial of reality) and a cinema on the right – a gigantic black blockhouse next to a bus station. At the Porte de Pantin, after having left the Avenue Jean-Jaurès bordered on one side by a Hôtel Mercure and on the other by Jean Nouvel's frightful Philharmonie, you find yourself in a no man's land, passing beneath the Périphérique, crossing the slip roads and tram lines, bypassing an inaccessible green space planted with grass and little Christmas trees. This path is still possible without danger, but further on, at the Porte de la Chapelle, the landscape is indescribable: the Périphérique, the bridge where the railway from the Gare de l'Est meets that from the Gare du Nord, and the ramps of the A1 and A3 motorways together form such an obstacle that it is a rare bird who risks crossing on foot from the Rue de la Chapelle to Saint-Denis.

At the Porte d'Ivry where I stopped for a moment, the traffic flow is much weaker, and the dominant impression is not chaos but concrete housing. The poor but dignified buildings of the Avenue Maurice-Thorez open onto the Place Jean-Ferrat, a large square whose centre is marked by a tired larch tree (according to the notice, a liberty tree planted for the centenary of 1789). The right-hand side of the place still contains down-market shops – halal butcher, pizzeria, Lycamobile – while on the left, at the foot of the twenty-storey towers, life insurance and white goods are signs of modernity. To the Paris side, the place is bordered by the Périphérique. On the corner, a large building of concrete and faux brick triumphantly bears the omnipresent syntagm 'BNP Paribas'. It is not enough for this banking establishment to have disfigured the Maison Dorée on the Boulevard des Italiens, a masterpiece of romantic architecture, or to have made countless Paris crossroads ugly with its greenish premises – it also has to impose itself in the banlieue, as here or at the Grands Moulins de Pantin, where it subjects a landscape worthy of Doisneau to its icy profitability. Between the Périphérique and the Boulevard des Maréchaux, which bears here the name of Masséna, you cross the ZAC Bédier.[1] How did the respected medievalist Joseph Bédier come to be enlisted for this purpose? His name only appears on a tiny street, off the Place du Docteur-Yersin – the disciple of Pasteur who discovered the plague bacillus, *Yersinia pestis* – another trace of medieval Paris. The pride of the ZAC is an immense office building on the Avenue de la Porte-d'Ivry. The signboard indicates that its architects are J.-M. Ibos and M. Vitart, former students and associates of Nouvel, known for creations that bear the same mark as their teacher, a concern for the façade. In this case, as represented on the signboard, the façade will have a uniform repetition of tall and narrow openings. This ZAC once again misses the opportunity for a harmonious junction between centre and periphery by way of a carefully woven urban fabric.

On the Boulevard Masséna, at the corner between the Avenue d'Ivry and the Rue Nationale, I discover a kind of relic, the former Panhard & Levassor works. The essentials of this three-level structure have been preserved, solid stone below and brick on the two upper floors. A plaque indicates: 'Here the automobile industry was born in 1891.' These are the walls from which so many marvels emerged, such as the large Dynamic saloon of 1937, with its headlights protected by a grille, three seats in front and the steering wheel in the middle. Or the little Dyna whose engine made a strange noise like a saucepan cooking, but which won the prize at Le Mans each year for its 'performance'. During the First World War, Panhard & Levassor, like Citroën and Renault, employed workers brought from Indochina, or recruited in China, to replace Frenchmen sent to the front. This is said to be the origin of the Chinese quarter in the 13th arrondissement, which grew in the 1970s with the arrival of the 'boat people'.

La Dynamic Panhard-Levassor, 1937.

The Avenue d'Ivry runs along the eastern side of this Chinatown, which continues across the Dalle des Olympiades. It is less busy than the neighbouring Avenue de Choisy, but there are several red and gold restaurants, and Chinese supermarkets in front of which old women sell bunches of aromatic herbs on upturned crates. It ends at the junction with the Rue de Tolbiac, the segment of a long ring road which leaves the Seine at the Pont de Tolbiac and returns at the Pont Mirabeau – or, if you prefer, from Léo Malet to Guillaume Apollinaire. Its aim was to link and open up the communes annexed in 1860 – Ivry, Gentilly, Montrouge, Vanves, Vaugirard and Grenelle. It bears the names of forgotten battles, not all of which are reliably attested: Tolbiac (victory of Clovis over the Alamans), Alésia (Vercingetorix's defence against Caesar's siege), Vouillé (victory of the Franks over the Visigoths). The municipal authorities of the 1860s probably intended to assert the Gallic and

Frank origins of the country (only later, under the Third Republic, was the final segment of the road named Rue de la Convention). If it works perfectly well for traffic, it has not encouraged notable urban developments: along these streets there is little life, little that is picturesque; you just drive. Which is also true for its counterpart on the Right Bank: the Avenue Simon-Bolivar, the Rue des Pyrénées, the Avenue du Général-Michel-Bizot.

On the Rue de Tolbiac, a few metres from the crossroads with the Avenue d'Ivry and the Avenue de Choisy, a building in 1950s style houses the Archives d'Architecture du XXe Siècle. Fifty years ago this was the Marie-Lannelongue surgical unit, where I conducted experimental work on coronary arteries in a laboratory headed by the gruff but charming Michel Weiss, the only person to have trusted me when I maintained that it was possible to operate on blood vessels no thicker than a matchstick or two. I have a pleasant memory of nights spent watching the laboratory dogs, and discussing the state of the world with Weiss and the lab assistant, who was also named Michel. No one, or hardly anyone, believed that this experimental work could have clinical applications, but today operations of this kind are carried out every day at dozens of centres in France, and thousands across the world.

A little way on from this crossroads, the Avenue de Choisy opens to the right onto a haven: the large Square de Choisy, almost a real park, which dates from the Exposition Internationale of 1937. A fine brick building from the same period stands on one side of the garden: the Fondation Eastman, a dental care centre founded by George Eastman, the American philanthropist who invented both celluloid photographic film and the first portable camera, the Kodak ('press the button, we do the rest'). The fact that Kodak could go bankrupt and end up being bought out by a Taiwanese businessman is as amazing as the collapse of General Motors.

The garden is designed in the French style, with a grace created by a harmony of proportions between a body of water, wide lawns, and double rows of linden trees. In the 1980s it was home to a sculpture by Richard Serra, 'Clara Clara', consisting of two large curved plates of weathering steel that the spectator could walk between. It seems that this is to be brought out of storage and placed near Nouvel's Philharmonie, where a little beauty would not go amiss.

At the end of the Avenue de Choisy I reach the Place d'Italie, where the counterpoint to the flat façade of the town hall of the 13th arrondissement is a building by Kenzo Tange, the Grand Écran, today known as Italie Deux. Tange was a good architect in the 1960s; but here, this immense concave curtain wall, topped by a Meccano campanile lift, adds nothing to his fame. The place itself is a major traffic roundabout. Its central reservation is deserted, since only daring sprinters could reach it. It was in crossing the Place d'Italie that Giacometti was knocked down by a car and left with a limp for the rest of his life. The reservation is planted with Paulownias, as Ernst Jünger, a botanist among other things, mentions in his *Journal de guerre*. On 5 May 1943, Jünger passed here en route for the Eastman centre, to get treatment for his teeth: 'All these Paulownias on the Place d'Italie: an impression of precious aromatic oil burning on enchanted candelabras.'[2] The blue flowers of these candelabras are not enough to add charm to the Place d'Italie, which has even less of it than the Place de la Nation, another great roundabout along the Wall of the Farmers-General, but whose central reservation boasts Dalou's magnificent 'Triumph of the Republic'. The municipal authorities preferred the fat lady by the Morice brothers, which contributes to the ugliness of the Place de la République today. At the time Dalou was under a cloud. He had been a member of the artists' commission during the Commune, still an unpardonable offence in the 1880s. Later on he would sculpt other marvels in Paris, such as the pediment of the Grands Magasins Dufayel on the Rue de Clignancourt, the monument to Delacroix in the Luxembourg, and the recumbent figure on Blanqui's tomb in Père-Lachaise.

© Cléo Marelli

Dalou's recumbent figure of Blanqui in Père-Lachaise.

During the June Days of 1848, the site of the present Place d'Italie saw one of the most controversial events in this great insurrection of the Paris proletariat, who took up arms against the threat of being sent to Algeria as agricultural workers, or to the Sologne to drain the marshes. The *barrière* here was part of the Wall of the Farmers-General, which followed the present course of the Boulevard de l'Hôpital on one side and that of the Boulevard Blanqui on the other. Situated in the middle of the present place, this *barrière*, designed like the other fifty-two gates in the Wall by Claude-Nicolas Ledoux, was made up of two pavilions

© Charles Marville/BHVP/Roger Viollet

The Barrière d'Italie around 1850.

whose arched façades faced each other in perfect symmetry, with the customs offices between them. This is where the misfortunes of General Bréa began on 25 June, the third day of the battle. Having seized half of Paris in the first couple of days, the insurgents were now in full retreat, routed even on the Left Bank where they were chased by artillery fire from the Latin Quarter, the Panthéon, the Montagne Sainte-Geneviève and the Faubourg Saint-Marceau. Withdrawing to the *barrière*, several hundred insurgents took up position behind a barricade erected between the two pavilions. General Bréa reached the *barrière* at the head of a column of 2,000 men, and proposed to negotiate. The accounts are so discordant that it will never be possible to decide whether this was a ruse of war or came from a real concern not to add to the bloodshed. What is certain is that Bréa entered the insurgent camp and did not come out alive. He was killed along with his aide de camp in a house on the Route de Fontainebleau (today the Avenue d'Italie), on the Maison-Blanche side. Twenty-six supposed authors of this 'abominable infamy' were tried by a military court in January 1849. Most were given long prison sentences, and two of them, Daix and Lahr, condemned to death. For their execution, the guillotine was erected close to the Barrière d'Italie, surrounded by thousands of soldiers and twelve cannon.

In the history of 1848 in France, the June Days hold a singular and even paradoxical place. Tocqueville himself, who participated on the side of order, bears witness to the gigantism of the event:

> This June insurrection, the greatest and the strangest that had ever taken place in our history, or perhaps in that of any other nation: the greatest because for four days more than a hundred thousand men took part in it, and there were five generals killed; the strangest, because the insurgents were fighting without a battle cry, leaders, or flag, and yet they showed wonderful powers of coordination and a military expertise that astonished the most experienced officers.[3]

Yet this black moment remains little explored: the last monograph devoted to it dates from 1880. The fact is that no brilliant figure emerges from the crowd of anonymous workers who took up arms on 23 June. Whereas the Commune of 1871 had Vallès and Courbet, Louise Michel, Élisabeth Dmitrieff, Eugène Varlin and so many others, the insurrection of June 1848 offers no individual, nor any narrative, for the imagination to hold on to. We should therefore remember the names, and honour the memory, of those who were brought before the council of war for the Bréa affair: Daix, a day labourer; Guillaume Pierre, known as Barbiche, a thresher; Coutant, a cooper; Beaude, a cobbler; Monis, a sausage-maker; Goué, foreman in a tannery; Paris, a horse dealer; Quintin, a builder's apprentice;

Lebelleguy, a cotton-spinner; Naudin, a day labourer; Luc, an employee of the highways department; Moussel, a dock worker; Vappreaux the elder, a horse dealer; Vappreaux the younger, the same; Lahr, a builder; Nourrit, an upholsterer; Bussière, a jeweller, Chopart, a bookshop employee; and Nuens, a clockmaker.[4]

CHAPTER 2

There are a number of possible itineraries from the Place d'Italie towards the centre, the most noisy and busy of these being the Boulevard de l'Hôpital. An imaginative effort is needed to appreciate how this used to cross one of the poorest backwaters of the city, a district of brigands and rag-pickers in which Jean Valjean and Cosette kept away from the world, sheltering in the Gorbeau hovel, 'a kind of dilapidated lean-to used by vegetable sellers as a store'. From still remoter times, there remains the porch of the Salpêtrière, now framed by the overhead Métro, and behind it the octagonal dome of the chapel, a masterpiece by Libéral Bruant dating from the 1670s.

In 1955 I spent the summer term at the Salpêtrière, as an intern under Henri Mondor. It was the last year before this lively little man retired, and he was still taking the stairs two at a time. The interns stood at the back when the master visited: some fifty or more individuals chatted their way through the immense communal wards with their three rows of beds, one against each wall and another in the middle. It was impossible to see or hear anything – the professors and registrars were much too far away – let alone see the patient being examined. Mondor was a prestigious figure, the author of treatises on surgery, a specialist on Mallarmé, and a grower of roses... In those days it was still possible for a surgeon to be all these things, but it was better to keep oneself in good health than be treated in these hospitals that had changed little from the time of Ambroise Paré.

From the Place d'Italie I could also take the Avenue des Gobelins to the church of Saint-Médard, then continue up the Montagne Sainte-Geneviève by the Rue Mouffetard as far as the Panthéon, a trajectory that follows the historic axis of the Faubourg Saint-Marceau, when the Rue Mouffetard ran from the Rue de la Contrescarpe as far as the Barrière d'Italie. At the time, as Balzac wrote in *The Commission in Lunacy*, the 12th arrondissement was

> the poorest quarter of Paris, that in which two-thirds of the population lack firing in winter, which leaves most brats at the gate of the Enfants-Trouvés, which sends most beggars to the poorhouse, most rag-pickers to the street corners, most decrepit old folks to bask against the walls on which the sun shines, most delinquents to the police courts.

Even after the upheavals of the Haussmann cuttings (the Boulevards Saint-Marcel, Arago, Blanqui), the Faubourg Saint-Marcel remained in the 1950s a working-class quarter, with factories such as Delahaye, which still made sports cars, the Say sugar refinery, the Sudac compressed-air plant... But as the arrondissement was a communist stronghold it was one of the first to be 'renovated', and with particular brutality (as likewise the 20th arrondissement, for the same reason). It is no longer possible to repeat the '*Les Misérables* walk' that I did with my father on Sunday mornings, to look for traces of the Gorbeau hovel, follow Marius dreaming of Cosette on the Rue du Champ-de-l'Alouette, discover Mère Grégoire's bar on the Rue Croulebarbe, whose customers included Chateaubriand, La Fayette, Véranger and the young Victor Hugo. (My father, though an immigrant naturalized in 1945, knew Paris and Hugo very well.)

To leave the Place d'Italie, I choose a more roundabout route that leads to an urban ghost, both buried and still present: the Bièvre and its valley. The Bièvre is a little river whose source is at Guyancourt in the Yvelines. It crosses Jouy-en-Josas, Bièvres, Antony, Cachan, Gentilly, and reaches Paris at the Poterne des Peupliers beneath the Boulevard Kellermann. Its route through Paris has been buried since 1912, and integrated into the city's drainage system. From the seventeenth century, however, trades developed along the river that required large amounts of water: tanneries, taweries, dyers, all activities seen as diseased. In Huysmans's words:

> Deprived of its clothing of grass and its lines of trees, it was forced to set to work and exhaust itself in the unpleasant tasks demanded of it ... It became tawed, and day and night washes the offal from flayed skins, macerates the piles of fleeces and raw leather, submits to the pinching of alum, the biting of lime and caustic.[1]

The Bièvre in the 1860s.

© Charles Marville/Musée Carnavalet/Roger Viollet

17

But if the Bièvre has disappeared from the surface, its route is still well known. It follows first of all the line of the Rue Vergniaud – it was from here that in winter floods the river spread its waters over a marsh whose ice, preserved under straw, gave its name to the Rue de la Glacière. The Bièvre then passes beneath the Boulevard Blanqui, encloses the public garden of Square René-Le Gall between two branches, flows under the Boulevard Arago, reaches the Jardin des Plantes and debouches into the Seine near the Pont d'Austerlitz. But this is only a partial outlet. In the fifteenth century, the monks of the Saint-Victor abbey (on

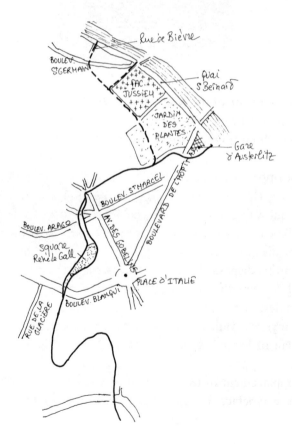

Typography of street names.

the present site of the Mutualité) diverted the course of the river in order to turn their mills. This 'canal of the Victorins' almost dried up the natural course of the river, and ended up joining the present line of the Rue de Bièvre to reach the Seine opposite Notre-Dame.

Formerly known as the Boulevard d'Italie, the Boulevard Blanqui was given its present name in 1905, at the time of the Bloc des Gauches, by way of homage to 'le Vieux', who spent his last years at no. 25, in a room on the fifth floor put at his disposal by a friend. (The plaques on the boulevard describe Blanqui as a 'politician' – precisely what he most despised. Not far away, Pascal is called a 'philosopher and mystic', while Stendhal, in the 20th arrondissement, is a 'man of letters'. It is not just the text on these plaques that is inappropriate. We should protest – at least I do – at the replacement of the old enamel plaques, with their fine Bodoni typeface, by tin plaques printed in wretched stick characters.)

Blanqui was freed in 1879 from the Clairvaux prison where he had spent seven years, condemned to a life sentence for his participation in the insurrection of 31 October 1870 against the government of 'national defence'. From his room on the boulevard, he wrote a long letter to Georges Clemenceau, who had campaigned for his release. Blanqui saw Clemenceau as a figure of hope, and his letter reads as if passing the torch: 'Become the man of the future, the leader of the revolution. It has not been able to find one since 1830. Fortune has now provided one, do not take him away.'[2] This reads very strangely for us, knowing what Clemenceau subsequently became.

The building at no. 25 – on the corner with the pretty Rue du Moulin-des-Près, which rises towards La Butte-aux-Cailles – today bears the violet and pink colours of a Hôtel Mercure. The plaque remains that recalls in suitably strong terms the illustrious inhabitant who was taken from here to Père-Lachaise followed by 100,000 Parisians.

On the opposite pavement, at the corner of the Rue Abel-Hovelacque where our friends at Éditions de la Découverte work, is the Estienne school that trained several generations in the book trade, and whose students included the young Robert Doisneau. Further on, the Boulevard Blanqui makes an angle just after the Corvisart Métro station with its fine brick façade. The Rue Corvisart (named after Napoleon's personal physician) descends gently towards the course of the Bièvre and a small quarter unique in the heart of Paris: here you have the sense of being in a valley, where chance and certain souls sensitive to place have combined varied architectural styles, with a wood and an old château, the whole forming a *paysage composé*, to use the expression from the time of Nicolas Poussin.

The Square René-Le Gall (a municipal councillor in the 13th arrondissement, shot on 7 March 1942) dates from

1938. It lies beneath the Rue Croulebarbe, which is bordered by a high retaining wall. After walking through a play area, as usual not very pretty – poorly designed swings and toboggans, painted in glaring colours, since it is an established fact that children have no taste – I enter a piece of woodland that seems almost wild, as the gardeners have taken care to let it grow with the least constraint possible. Then, between the edge of this forest and the side of the square, marked by the walls of the Mobilier National, in the centre of the open space we find a 'creation' – in the sense that Encelade's copse at Versailles is a creation. There is a topiary quincunx of box bushes, with roses in the middle: four open semi-cylindrical arbours frame a small obelisk of raw stone. The roses climb over the arbours and embrace the obelisk. To give an idea of the charm of the place, you have to recall one of those painters who were not landscape artists but painted almost by chance a single landscape – I have in mind the Villa Medici gardens by Velasquez, or

Jacques-Louis David, The Luxembourg, *1794.*

David's view of the Luxembourg, painted from the cell where he awaited the guillotine after Thermidor.

To leave the Square René-Gall you have the choice between two stairways, each with two flights of steps. One leads up to the Rue des Cordeliers, and the other to the Rue Croulebarbe. On both sides, the ramp is supported by a high wall inscribed with strange stone medallions, pebbles and shells, in which you can discern human and animal figures. At the foot of the ramps, heavy stone balls punctuate this remarkable ensemble, the work of an architect by the name of Jean-Charles Moreau.

'Remarkable' is not too strong a word. Between the world wars there was very little new building in Paris, apart from the sorry extension of the Boulevard Haussmann from the Rue de la Chausée-d'Antin to the Rue Drouot, which destroyed in its wake the Passage du Thermomètre and the Passage du Baromètre, haunts of the Surrealists in the 1920s. But this epoch did leave several fine gardens laid out in the peripheral quarters – the Parc de Choisy, as we have seen; the garden where the Rue Sorbier broadens out at Ménilmontant; the Square Séverine near the Porte de Bagnolet – along with two masterpieces: the Square René-Le Gall and the Square du Chapeau-Rouge, whose terraces continue along the Boulevard Sérurier above Le Pré-Saint-Gervais, overlooking the whole of Paris's north-eastern suburbs and, in clear weather, the heights of the Montmorency forest behind them.

The stairway on the Croulebarbe side leads me up to the building of the Mobilier National, one of the major works of Auguste Perret in Paris. Its central courtyard is approached via a structure that might be called a porch (though with no thickness), an arcade (but without an arch), or perhaps a colonnade: two pairs of columns in fluted concrete, slightly tapered, bearing a thin convex architrave. At the foot of each pair of columns rests a stone lion. This light and almost fantastic entrance balances the severity of the three sides of the courtyard and their large blind openings, which was a necessity: the building is a storehouse for furniture, and furniture is stored away from the light. (How can it have been proposed – let alone accepted – that in the Bibiothèque Nationale books are kept in glass towers and readers in cellars?)

On the other side of the Rue Croulebarbe we have the first skyscraper built in Paris, in 1960: twenty-six storeys, interrupted by a terrace on the sixth floor designed to create a visual relationship with the streets behind it, higher than the Rue Croulebarbe which nestles in the valley. The frame of steel tubes is so well designed that the hostility shown at the time of the building's construction has disappeared. Today it is part and parcel of the neighbourhood.

I leave the valley of the Bièvre by the Rue Gustave-Geffroy, which rises in hairpins towards the Avenue des Gobelins. (Gustave Geffroy wrote the first biography of Blanqui – *L'Enfermé*, 1897 – and it was while visiting Blanqui's prison on Belle-Île that he made the acquaintance of Claude Monet, becoming one of his main champions. The reason for Geffroy having a street named after him here is that Clemenceau appointed him administrator of the Mobilier National.) While climbing, you glimpse the 'Château of Queen Blanche', better seen from the Rue des Gobelins (formerly the Rue de Bièvre). This authentic fifteenth-century building probably has nothing to do with Queen Blanche, who might be either the widow of Saint Louis or else Blanche de Navarre, wife of Philippe VI de Valois.[3] And the legend that this is where the famous 'Bal des Ardents' took place (the courtiers of the mad Charles VI, covered with tar and feathers for a masked ball, burned alive in a fire) is equally unfounded.

Then, through the little Rue des Marmousets, I pass from silence to turmoil as I come out on the Boulevard Arago. This boulevard gains from familiarity. By car and even on a bicycle nothing leaps to the eye, but on foot it's a different matter. Its chestnut trees are among the earliest in Paris, they come into leaf at the beginning of April and take autumn colours in the month of August. The buildings in the background are in the style wrongly named after Haussmann, though they date from the 1880s, their façades often bearing their date and the name of their architect. (The streets, which actually are the product of Haussmann, are often confused with the period of construction. Not so many buildings were erected under Haussmann as is commonly believed.4) Mixed in with these are some buildings from the 1960s, and picturesque *hôtels particuliers*. At no. 65, the Cité Fleurie is a collection of artists' studios also dating from the 1880s, which at various times had both Gauguin and Modigliani as tenants, and today has Jérôme Saint-Loubert Bié, who created the design for the La Fabrique editions nearly twenty years ago.

The Boulevard Arago then crosses the Rue de la Santé, the boundary between the 13th and 14th arrondissements. This corner was the place of public executions between 1909 and 1939, after which they took place within the prison. Opposite the main gate of the prison, reinforced and always closed, low buildings and a café with the sign La Bonne Santé were replaced in the 1960s by an aparment block. At the corner of the Rue Jean-Dolent, the prison wall bears a plaque with the names of eighteen *résistants* executed here after being judged and condemned by the Sections Spéciales, tribunals created in 1941 by interior minister Pierre Pucheu and justice minister Joseph Barthélemy. No doubt we shall have to wait another fifty years for a plaque to indicate that it was within these same walls that members of the FLN were guillotined after being condemned to death by military tribunals during the Algerian War, under a procedure similar to that of the Sections Spéciales.

Today, visitors to the Santé enter through a tiny gatehouse on the opposite side from the main gate, on the short Rue Messier. A few years ago, I came this way several times to see a friend imprisoned here. It was winter, and from a caravan on the opposite pavement, nuns offered coffee to poor people waiting in the cold. Among all the families in the queue, I never saw a single white person. Nor were there many among the guards who controlled the entrances. As in the Paris hospitals, subaltern jobs in the prison system are often filled by West Indians.

After long-running rumours of its imminent demise, the Santé was finally demolished in January 2016. It is the last in a long series of prisons to have disappeared since the most famous of their number – the Bastille – was dismantled in the summer of 1789. The others included the Abbaye prison, near the church of Saint-Germain-des-Près, where the September massacres began; the Force, on the Rue Saint-Antoine at the corner of the present Rue Mahler, where Claude-Nicolas Ledoux was imprisoned (he would come out alive) and later the four sergeants of La Rochelle, guillotined on the Place de Grève on 21 September 1822 for plotting against the restored Bourbon monarchy; the Madelonnettes, a women's prison on the Rue Turbigo, where the Lycée Turgot now stands; Sainte-Pélagie, between the Rue de la Clef and the Rue du Puits-de-l'Ermite, a political prison under the Restoration and the July monarchy, through which all the opposition leaders passed, as well as Gérard de Nerval, who speaks of it in a poem:

In Sainte-Pélagie,
Under this lengthy reign
Where I lived in captivity,
Dreamy and pensive...[5]

There was also Clichy, a debtors' prison that stood at no. 68 on the street of the same name, where the inmates were locked up and maintained at the cost of their creditors; and the Petite Roquette, a hexagonal panopticon for women that was not demolished until 1974.

After the Santé, at the corner with the Rue du Faubourg-Saint-Jacques, there is a bare plinth. Before the war, it carried a statue of François Arago, opposite the gardens of the Observatoire, of which he was for a long time the director. An inscription indicates that the statue was destroyed by the Vichy government, and that in 1994, Jan Dibbets, a Dutch conceptual artist, replaced it with an 'imaginary monument, made from medallions marked with the astronomer's name, fixed to the ground along the course of the Paris meridian that crosses this place at the statue's plinth' – a far better homage than the duds contemporary statuary generally produces. François Arago was an ambiguous figure: a great scientist, an opponent of the July monarchy, an active campaigner for the abolition of slavery in 1848, and indeed a republican icon. But he was also minister of war in the provisional government at the start of the Second Republic, and personally directed the artillery barrage on the Latin Quarter during the June Days, hurling abuse at the insurgent workers who had attacked the Republic and the result of universal suffrage.

From this plinth, passing the Institut d'Astrophysique, the Société des Missions Évangéliques and the Arago clinic – summarizing in just a few metres this site's scientific, theological and medical achievements – I approach the Lion de Belfort on the Place Denfert-Rochereau from behind. At the time of Chateaubriand and Balzac, this place was known as the Barrière d'Enfer. The barriers of the Wall of the Farmers-General – gates in the customs wall – bore either the name of the road that started from them (Italie, Neuilly), or sometimes that of the road leading to them (La Chapelle, Maine and Rochechouart). There was indeed a Rue d'Enfer leading to the barrier, but what precise hell did this refer to? Perhaps the street in question had been the *via Inferior*, when the Rue Saint-Jacques was the *via Superior*: Inferior, Infera, d'Enfer... Nor do I know whether the Barrière d'Enfer was chosen as a place of homage to Colonel Denfert-Rochereau by an accidental homonym, or whether we should suspect a trace of farcical spirit among the municipal councillors of the 1880s.

Crossed by traffic in all directions, is the space around the Lion a real square or simply a great crossroads? To be a square, it seems to me, there should be more closed space than open, more buildings than emptiness, a junction of streets, green or other spaces. But whatever the definition, Paris is not a city of squares, as Louis Chevalier notes:

What are our squares worth beside the squares of Rome – with their brilliant fountains, their Michelangelo marbles covered with dust? [He should have said 'Bernini', as I can see no Michelangelo statues on the Roman fountains. – E.H.] The Place de la République and its great bronze lady, with the barracks behind; the Bastille, immense and empty, peaked by a column and only needing an elephant; the Concorde, likewise decked out with an obelisk...[6]

Is Denfert-Rochereau a real square, then? Yes, despite everything, as it is strongly centred, structured, organized by the two pavilions of the former *barrière* that give it meaning, and make it more than a crossroads swept by the flow of traffic.

These two square-fronted buildings stand opposite one another, symmetrical in relation to the avenue that has successively been called Orléans, Maréchal-Leclerc, and more recently, in its short initial segment, after Colonel Rol-Tanguy – who prepared the insurrection of 19 August 1944 in the basement of the westerly pavilion. In this building, the Paris highways department now studies road surface materials, the different types of paving and asphalt. The opposite building houses the Inspection Générale des Carrières de Paris, and the door giving access to the Catacombes is also here. The façades of the two buildings are examples of Claude-Nicolas Ledoux's classicism, the entrance framed by two pairs of columns whose design appears simple at first sight – a cylinder broken by three large rectangular blocks. A second look shows that the cylinder is slightly tapered, and that the three blocs decline in width from bottom to top. This solidity and severity – ritual words in relation to Ledoux – go well, I think, with Guimard's Art Nouveau ironwork for the Métro entrance next to the westerly pavilion. In front of this, on the pavement, the trailer of Madame Ranah, clairvoyant and medium, along with a hut selling waffles, are the remains of a travelling fair that often used to be held here, and where as a little boy I tried to see the knickers of girls flying up on the swings.

Each of these two pavilions is backed by gardens dating, like the Lion, from the 1880s. Their design remains uncertain and their vegetation poor, but they have a certain charm due to their dilapidated monuments built at the start of the Third Republic. Behind the Métro station, in the garden that bears Ledoux's name, a little pyramid surrounded by sad-looking characters is a monument to Ludovic Trarieux,

*Place Denfert-Rochereau: Ledoux
pavilion and Métro entrance.*

founder of the Ligue des Droits de l'Homme at the time of the Dreyfus affair. The adjacent garden, on the other side of the Rue Froidevaux (a fireman who died on duty), also reminds us of the name of a neoclassical architect, Jacques Antoine, creator among other things of the Monnaie and the École des Ponts et Chaussées on the Rue des Saints-Pères. The central monument has lost its statue, but the plinth is decked on each side with a bronze bas-relief illustrating an aspect of the life of François-Vincent Raspail. On the northern side he is shown as doctor to the poor, his hat in his hand, taking the pulse of a dying man surrounded by a grieving family; on the southern side he is the political leader, with the same hat but now on his head, showing the way with a broad gesture to insurgents armed with muskets. I had considered Raspail a sympathetic character, who seemed to me more like Blanqui than Arago. Passing the Rue de Sévigné, I always looked up at no. 5 where a plaque indicates that this 'promoter of universal suffrage' – who was born in Carpentras on 24 January 1794 and died at Arcueil on 7 January 1878 – 'gave free care to the sick from

1840 to 1848'. But I changed my mind after reading, in Gustave Lefrançais's *Souvenirs d'un révolutionnaire*, that Raspail owned a building from which he evicted tenants who did not pay their rent – Lefrançais himself being one of them.[7]

Behind the Catacombes pavilion, on the Square de l'Abbé-Migne (a nineteenth-century churchman and philologist), a small column bears the bas-relief effigy of Charlet, engraver and lithographer of the Romantic era, who played a major role in propagating the legend of Napoleon. His was a character of the same stature as Béranger – in *Les Misérables* we read that 'if Virgil haunted the bars of Rome, David d'Angers, Balzac and Charlet dined in the cheap restaurants of Paris'.

To the east side, the square is bordered by the station of the RER B (when I was at school, this was called the 'ligne de Sceaux'), the oldest in Paris still completely preserved, which is very fortunate as, with its undulating façade enlivened by pilasters and its three large doors, it nicely closes the space between the Avenue René-Coty and the Boulevard Saint-Jacques.

The buildings around the place are more opulent-looking, especially on the side facing Montparnasse. To the south, between an Indian restaurant and a lawyer's office, is the Hôtel Floridor, which, even if it has only a single star in the guidebooks, is dear to friends of Walter Benjamin, who lived here in 1934–5, between his stays at the Palace on the Mabillon crossroads and at 23 Rue Bénard, two steps from Denfert-Rochereau.

I happen to have a personal relationship with the Lion. More precisely, I owe him a debt, as he is bound up with a decisive turning point in my existence. In 1981, I was living by the Parc Montsouris and had worked for nearly twenty years in a cardiac surgery unit at the Laennec hospital near

Le Bon Marché. One night, called out on an emergency, I found myself waiting at the traffic lights of the Place Denfert-Rochereau, which take a long time to turn green. Looking at the Lion, it suddenly struck me as obvious that I would not continue the same existence for a further twenty years. That night, for the first time, I thought about ending my surgical career, changing my life, and leaving a world that still seemed foreign to me despite the many years I had spent in it. So much so that since that time, whenever I pass the Lion, I mentally raise my hat and thank him for having steered me towards a new life.

Before Haussmann's cutting of the Boulevard Saint-Michel, a long road led from the Pont Saint-Michel to the Barrière d'Enfer, parallel to the Rue Saint-Jacques. Certain segments of this route still remain, more or less modified, while others have been absorbed as part of modern streets. Starting from the bridge, the very ancient Rue de la Harpe is today cluttered with a profusion of pizzerias, kebab shops and Greek restaurants. (When I was a student, the Saint-Séverin quarter was deserted in the evenings, and there were only two places open to eat, one on the Rue de la Huchette, which I believe was called Chez Papille, and the other on the Rue des Prêtres-Saint-Séverin, run by Yugoslavs and decorated with large photos of Mihailovic, head of the Serbian resistance and Tito's rival.) The Rue de la Harpe then took the present-day route of the Boulevard Saint-Michel, from the Rue Racine up to the Place Saint-Michel (now Edmond-Rostand). There it took the name Rue d'Enfer, skirted the Luxembourg, and followed the present-day Rue Henri-Barbusse. From the Observatoire crossroads, the Rue d'Enfer continued towards the *barrière* in a final segment that is today the Avenue Denfert-Rochereau.

Descending the Rue d'Enfer from the *barrière* (on, in present-day terms, the Avenue Denfert-Rochereau from the square of that name), the wall on the left used to be that of the Marie-Thérèse infirmary founded by Mme de Chateaubriand to take in elderly widows and priests. In Book 36 of his *Mémoires d'outre-tombe*, written here in May 1833, Chateaubriand, then aged sixty-five, meditated on the improvements made to the site:

> My trees are of various kinds. I have planted twenty-three cedars of Lebanon and two druid oaks: they mock their master with his slender longevity . . . I have not selected these trees as I did at the Vallée-aux-Loups in memory of places I have visited. He who delights in memories preserves his hopes, but when one lacks children, youth and homeland what attachment can one have to trees whose leaves, flowers and fruits are no longer mysterious symbols used to count the days of illusion? . . . Moreover my trees scarcely know if they serve as a calendar for my pleasures or as death certificates for my years; they grow each day, as I shrink; they marry themselves to those of the Enfants-Trouvés enclosure and the Boulevard d'Enfer which envelop me. I see not one house; I would be less divorced from the world six hundred miles from Paris.

The entrance to this site, still occupied by a charitable institution, is closed on the side of the avenue. From the Boulevard Raspail the gardens can be admired through a gate, or better, from the path that winds its way around the Fondation Cartier. The cedars are still there, the most impressive one being almost integrated into the building's impeccable glass façade, built by Jean Nouvel in 1994.

Returning to the Avenue Denfert-Rochereau, I pass the wall of the Oeuvre des Jeunes Filles Aveugles and reach the front of the Saint-Vincent-de-Paul hospital. In the Romantic age this was still the Enfants-Trouvés: babies could be

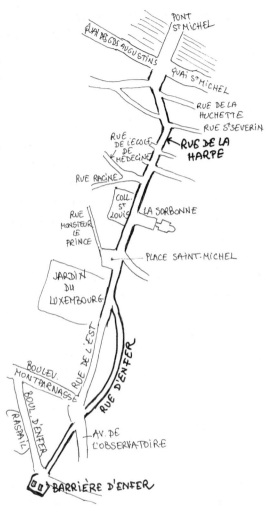

abandoned in the famous 'tower' described by Balzac. The mechanism was similar to what you see in a post office: a cylinder half-open and half-closed, which can be rotated to allow a package to be passed from one side of the wall to the other without the person depositing the infant being visible – or without it being possible to threaten the counter clerk with a pistol and force them to hand over the cash.

For me, this place is forever linked to the memory of a man who did far more than just work here; he spent the greatest part of his life in the place. Gilbert Huault was red-haired, not very tall, but of an imposing technical ability and moral stature. He invented a new discipline and developed it to a mature stage: that of neonatal resuscitation. Huault's unit was not a factory but the cutting edge of medical handicraft: everything was thought out, everything was perfect down to the last piece of bandage. For years, paediatric cardiac surgeons in Paris sent their patients to Huault: babies weighing three or four kilos were taken by a special ambulance to what was called the SVP. Huault was not an easy man, and I never recall seeing him laugh; in fact, he often bawled me out for not having fixed a catheter properly, or for leaving a drain partially blocked because the probe was too deeply inserted. He was never satisfied, and although he was neither older nor better qualified than me, he made a great impression. He helped hundreds of infants survive, trained generations of paediatric resuscitators, and never took time off. Perhaps he had to be rather neurotic to lead such an existence, but if there is such a thing as divine justice, then Gilbert Huault surely has a good place in heaven.

The hospital has been closed since 2011, the courtyard invaded by vegetation, and the metal uprights of the portico rusted. Entering through the school of midwifery, you can walk through to the back wall that separates the hospital from the Rue Boissonnade, one of the loveliest in Montparnasse. All these buildings are due to be demolished and an 'eco-neighbourhood' built in their place – a disturbing prospect.

Opposite the hospital is the Rue Cassini, which skirts the façade of the Observatoire – the work of Claude Perrault, whose brother Charles was the famous author of fairy tales. Claude was both a doctor and an architect, and a good one at that: he was entrusted with the Louvre colonnade after Bernini's plans were rejected by Colbert. As for Cassini, this is the name of a whole dynasty of astronomers who were directors of the Observatoire for more than a century.

12 Rue Cassini is a 1930s Art Nouveau building, where I lived with my parents from just after Liberation until I reached eighteen. From our duplex on the fifth and sixth floors you could see the gardens of a convent on the Avenue Denfert-Rochereau where the nuns grew their vegetables, and look south as far as Gentilly and Ivry. The day's rhythm was set by the great Observatoire clock, which no doubt gave me my mania for punctuality. I spent my lycée years there (there was no middle school at that time), initially at Lycée Montaigne, which I reached via the paths of the Observatoire, continuing below the Parthenon friezes reproduced on the brick building that housed the Institut d'Art et d'Archéologie, then past the pharmacy faculty and finally the École Coloniale (called the 'Colo'), built in Moorish style. After the *quatrième* class, the Lycée Montaigne students went on to Louis-le-Grand, which was not yet the elitist school it later became. To get there, I took either the Rue Saint-Jacques or the Boulevard Saint-Michel, but when it rained I caught the 38 bus – its platform open at the back (so that even if it was full, policemen or firemen could cling on to the rails), with a conductor who slipped the tickets into a little metal machine he held against his stomach, stamping them by turning a handle whose sound I can still recall.

The Rue Cassini has changed little since that time. On the Faubourg-Saint-Jacques side, a number of *hôtels particuliers* from around 1900 give it a picturesque look, even if the building at no. 1 is no longer that where Balzac lived from 1828 to 1837 and wrote a large part of *La Comédie humaine*. I remember that Bernard Lajarrige, a good supporting actor in French films of the 1950s, lived in one of these *hôtels*. He played a policeman in *The Trip Across Paris*, and his beautiful daughter excited the gang of adolescents to which I belonged.

From the Rue Cassini, a short zigzag via Rue Faubourg-Saint-Jacques leads to the Rue Méchain, where the Union printing works used to occupy no. 13. I often accompanied my father when he went there to see to the printing of the classics he published around 1950, before he moved on to art books. It was quite a spectacle to watch the typographers at work. Using tweezers they would pick up the lead characters arranged in their box, and compose lines at an amazing speed. This open wooden box contained a set of compartments, one per font. Inclined at 45 degrees, these contained the capital or 'upper case' letters above, and the small or 'lower case' letters below, terms still used even now that typesetting is done by computer. To change fonts, for example from Garamond to Didot, the box was changed.

The Union printing works has a whole story attached to it. Founded in 1910 by two Russian immigrants, Chalit and Snégaroff, it initially served the very active Russian community in Paris, and was supposedly used by Plekhanov and Lenin. It then moved into book printing, along with publications of the modernist movement. Apollinaire had his first *Calligrammes* printed there, Léonce Rosenberg the *Bulletin de l'Effort moderne*, the Surrealists *Le Surréalisme au service de la révolution* and the magazine *Minotaure*, while Jacques Schiffrin printed the Pléiade series. After the war Aimé Maeght and many of the major Paris galleries entrusted the Union with their books and magazines.

I was fond of Chalit and Snégaroff, their courtesy, their Russian accents, their welcome. These two characters from another age, after making sure in the mornings that everything was under control on the Rue Méchain, went on to spend the rest of their day – so my father said – playing chess in Montparnasse. The Union closed its doors in 1990, when most of Parisian printing had already left for the ban-lieue. One of the last survivors of the golden age, Jacques London (also an émigré Russian Jew), whose works were on the Rue de la Grange-Batelière and printed the covers for La Fabrique, has just closed its doors.

From the Rue Cassini, the Avenue de l'Observatoire duly follows the Paris meridian. On the left side, a plaque recalls that Jean Cavaillès was arrested there before being shot in February 1944. Georges Canguilhem, also a major figure in the Resistance, wrote a short text in which he tells how his friend, this philosopher of mathematics, founded the move-ment Libération-Sud together with D'Astier de la Vigerie, and subsequently the military network Cahors.[8] 'Imagine one of your young professors', Canguilhem addressed his students,

appearing dressed in overalls in the submarine base that the Kriegsmarine was building at Lorient. Do you think that behind the mask of a simple attentive worker, Car-rière, in other words Cavaillès, could not but be aware that his life was at stake? . . . This was the man that stu-dents like you might have had as your teacher today, but whom they do not have, because he was a man such as I have sought to depict for you.

Opposite this black plaque, the right side of the Avenue de l'Observatoire was formerly bordered by a long wall that hid the buildings of the Port-Royal maternity hospital. For years, I could decipher here an inscription in black paint: 'Fighting for Défense de la France is fighting for liber-ation' (*Défense de la France* was a resistance movement, but above all a newspaper with the largest print-run of the underground press; it became *France-Soir* in 1944). Today, the truncated corner formed by the Avenue de l'Observatoire, the start of the Rue Henri-Barbusse and the Boulevard Port-Royal is occupied by an extension of the maternity hospital, the work of the same architects who designed the new Les Halles canopy, Patrick Berger and Jacques Anziutti: unrelieved repetition of verticals, spandrels in imitation marble, yellowy door-frames, botched details. The builders of today's hospitals often have marvels close at hand: the architects of the new Saint-Louis hospital had before their eyes every morning the wings dating from Henri IV; those who built the extension of the Cochin hospital could see opposite them the Val-de-Grâce constructed in the days of Anne of Austria; and here, at Port-Royal, the architects were only a few metres from the buildings of the abbey and monastery. I do not mean that they should have resorted to pastiche or eclecticism, but they had a challenge to meet, a possible source of inspiration such as Velasquez was for Manet, or Saint-Simon for Proust. One may always dream.

The maternity hospital is situated alongside the big Observatoire intersection. Crossing this, I have in mind the ending of Balzac's *Ferragus*, in which the former head of the Dévorants, at one time a fearsome character, is now a broken old man whose cane the boules players borrow to measure their throws. Between the south gate of the Luxembourg and the north gate of the Observatoire, Balzac writes, is

a space without a name, the neutral space of Paris. There, Paris is no longer; and there, Paris still lingers. The spot is a mingling of street, square, boulevard, fortification, garden, avenue, high-road, province and metropolis; certainly, all of that is to be found there, and yet the place is nothing of all that – it is a desert. Around this spot without a name stand the Enfants-Trouvés, the Bourbe, the

Cochin hospital, the Capucines, the La Rochefoucauld hospital, the deaf and dumb asylum, the hospital of the Val-de-Grâce; in short, all the vices and all the misfortunes of Paris find their asylum there. And (that nothing may lack in this philanthropic centre) Science there studies the tides and longitudes, Monsieur de Chateaubriand has erected the Marie-Therèse infirmary, and the Carmelites have founded a convent. The great events of life are represented by bells which ring incessantly through this desert – for the mother giving birth, for the babe that is born, for the vice that succumbs, for the toiler who dies, for the virgin who prays, for the old man shaking with cold, for genius self-deluded. And a few steps off is the cemetery of Montparnasse, where, hour after hour, the sorry funerals of the Faubourg Saint-Marceau wend their way.

On the esplanade between the Rue d'Assas and the Rue Notre-Dame-des-Champs, which is not asphalted, some of my friends still used to play boules only twenty years ago. On reflection, the places listed by Balzac are still there even if the names have changed, as if science, the church and the hospital had a gift of preservation – one that also extends to the surroundings here: the Boulevard de Port-Royal has remained the same as when my mother went to do her shopping here, and the Boulevard Montparnasse has kept its calm pavements and provincial shops as far as the Raspail crossroads.

The Boulevard Saint-Michel and the Rue d'Assas define a wide corner that opens towards the chestnut trees of the Observatoire's paths, which stretch as far as the eye can see through to the gates of the Luxembourg. On the Saint-Michel side are the station of the former 'ligne de Sceaux' with its pretty ironwork; the Beauvoir Hôtel, whose neon sign stands out in a famous night-time photo by Brassaï; the building of the CROUS [Centre Régionale d'Oeuvres Universitaires et Scolaires], constructed in the 1960s on the site of a small stadium where we used to go running when I was at the Lycée Montaigne. On the Rue d'Assas side you have La Closerie des Lilas, whose great days were before the war, even before the First World War, but whose terrace is still worth visiting outside of peak hours.

Two of the corners are marked by famous sculptures. In front of La Closerie, Marshal Ney brandishes his sabre, close to where he was shot in 1815. The creator of this heroic effigy, François Rude, was first a Bonapartist, and then a republican when he sculpted the recumbent figures of Godefroy Cavaignac in the Montmartre cemetery ('our Godefroy', not to be confused with his brother Louis Eugène, the general who butchered the insurgents of June 1848). On the Luxembourg side is a fountain that marks the entrance to the paths of the Observatoire, the 'Four Parts of the World', gracious spiralling figures bearing above them the celestial sphere. Carpeaux created this group just before his death, and it was Férmiet who sculpted the bronze horses and the turtles that shoot their jets of water towards the central motif. This pleasant halt in the shade of the chestnuts is not exceptional; fine Paris fountains are to be found in public gardens, such as the Médicis fountain in the Luxembourg, the elegant Quatre-Fleuves fountain designed by Visconti for the Square Louvois in front of the Bibliothèque Nationale, or again the Fontaine aux Lions that stands today at the entrance to the gardens of La Villette. On the paved streets and squares, on the other hand, I see nothing worthwhile, apart from the masterpiece by Tinguely and Niki de Saint Phalle in the Beaubourg complex. There are places that could do well with a fountain, such as the Place des Vosges, the Place des Victoires, the Place Vendôme – but the preference has been to install a king on horseback or an emperor on a column. And the modern fountains, from the Place de la Sorbonne via the Place Saint-German-des-Près to the Place Gambetta, are each more ridiculous than the last. Taking the short Rue du Val-de-Grâce, I come to the façade of the great church of that name. Anne of Austria entrusted its construction to Mansart, but the man was not accommodating and modified his plans as he went along, which caused delays and budget overruns, as we would say today. Claude Perrault said of Mansart that 'better ideas always came to him while working than those he had started off with, and often he had to repeat the same pieces two or three times', so much so that the work had hardly been started when it was removed from Mansart and entrusted to architects who were unworthy of it, first of all Lemercier, then Le Muet. (It was an attractive feature of seventeenth-century France, the existence of these stiff-necked characters such as François Mansart, Blaise Pascal, Nicolas Poussin.) If the church of Val-de-Grâce has a badly proportioned drum and dome – like Soufflot's Panthéon – this is undoubtedly bound up with the modifications made to Mansart's plan. And it seems to me that Balzac exaggerated a bit in referring at the start of *Old Goriot* to 'the silence that reigns in the streets shut in between the dome of the Panthéon and the dome of the Val-de-Grâce, two conspicuous public buildings which give a yellowish tone to the landscape and darken the whole district that lies beneath the shadow of their leaden-hued cupolas'.

From the semi-circular place in front of the Val-de-Grâce gate, I can see further down the Rue Saint-Jacques the square bell-tower of another church, Saint-Jacques-du-Haut-Pas. The two buildings are neighbours and almost contemporary, and yet opposite in every way. One is fat and the other thin, one ornate and rich, the other poor and bare, one built according to the rules, the other according to the builders' taste, even if Gittard, the architect of Saint-Sulpice, supervised the work and designed its façade. If the Val-de-Grâce is a Jesuit church – in the sense that it is built after the plan of the Gesù in Rome – Saint-Jacques-du-Haut-Pas is a Jansenist temple. The church is indeed bound up with the history of Jansenism: its foundation stone was laid by the Duchesse de Longueville, sister of the Grand Condé and illustrious protector of Port-Royal. Jansenist pilgrims would gather before the tomb of Duvergier de Hauranne, abbot of Saint-Cyran and a friend of Jansen, the spiritual advisor to the nuns of Port-Royal, who spent five years in prison and was only released on the death of Richelieu.

Just before reaching Saint-Jacques-du-Haut-Pas, the Rue des Ursulines opens to the right from the Rue Saint-Jacques. It boasts a very nice hall that was an art cinema during the golden age of Paris film around 1960s. It was in the Ursulines that I saw the first films of Jean Rouch, *Moi, un noir* and *Chronicle of a Summer*. At that time, art cinemas were almost all on the Left Bank. In the Latin Quarter, apart from the minuscule Champo (the other halls on the Rue Champollion were still theatres), you had further up on the Rue Victor-Cousin the Panthéon cinema that still exists, valiantly independent, and where I saw one morning in 1963 the preview of Chris Marker's *Le Joli Mai*. On the Place Saint-Sulpice, between the *mairie* and the Rue du Vieux-Colombier, there was a cinema whose name I forget (the Bonaparte?). In Montparnasse, there were two almost adjacent: the Raspail in a fine modernist building, and the Parnasse on the little Rue Jules-Chaplain, which still exists but is now the MK2 Parnasse. Here, each Thursday after the last screening, the owner asked impossible questions on cinema history, and the first to give the correct answer won a free ticket (apparently, when Truffaut was there, he took them all). A little further off, the Bertrand, on the street of that name, gave a bit of life to the sorry Duroc quarter.

On the Right Bank, if I'm not mistaken, there were only two art cinemas: the Mac-Mahon, closely associated with the New Wave, and the Studio 28 on the Rue Tholozé in Montmartre, famous for the scandal aroused by the screening of Buñuel's *L'Age d'or*. In the 1930s, the far-right leagues had attacked the cinema with cries of 'death to Jews' (Marie-Laure de Noailles, wife of the film's producer, was Jewish).

It was in these cinemas that my generation came to know the American cinema of the 1930s and '40s – Howard Hawks, John Huston, Frank Capra, Ernst Lubitsch – as well as the German and Soviet classics, the postwar Italians, not to mention such French directors as Jean Grémillon, Jean Renoir and Jean Vigo. Since this time, the concentration of film distribution and the proliferation of multiplexes has led to the closure of many of these independent cinemas run by cultured film-lovers.

That last sentence may be read as symptomatic: as the years pass, it is a natural tendency to believe that everything was better in the past; in other words, when we were young. I don't claim to be totally immune to this tendency to become a nostalgic old grouch, but it is not the only reason I no longer feel at home on the present Left Bank. A real decadence has struck the very heart of this area, between the Jardin des Plantes and the Rue du Bac, the Boulevard Montparnasse and the Seine. The basic reason for this is a transfer of population. When I lived on the Rue de la Montagne-Sainte-Geneviève in the late 1950s, workers still lived in the quarter, if often in small rooms on the top floor, with toilets on the landing. But they were there. Algerian workers stayed in weekly or monthly hotels between the Rue Maubert and the Seine, on the Rue Maître-Albert, the Rue Frédéric-Sauton, the Rue de Bièvre. Down-and-outs

colonized the Rue de la Contrescarpe and the Rue Mouffetard. (Those who don't believe me can read Jean-Paul
Clébert's excellent *Paris insolite*, published by Denoël in
1952.) When my father had his publishing house on the Rue
de Seine, overalls were as common in the local cafés as tweed
jackets. Then, starting in the 1960s, the great renovation
project launched by Malraux and continued by Pompidou
put up rents to levels that drove the working class from the
heart of the Left Bank, on their way to being pushed out of
Paris completely. (It is said that the Right Bank has suffered
the same fate, but this is not true: it is twice as large with
twice the population, and contains pockets of popular resistance that are slow and difficult to suppress.)

During this sociological upheaval, spread over many
years, events occurred that had the effect of securing the
Left Bank for commodity fetishism. Before May '68, the
Latin Quarter fully deserved its name. All the Paris students were concentrated there, in the Sorbonne, the law
faculty on the Place du Panthéon, the two medical facul-
ties and that of pharmacy – as well as the *grandes écoles*
that framed the Montagne Sainte-Geneviève – the École des
Mines, the École Normale Supérieure, the Polytechnique,
and the Beaux-Arts on the Quai Malaquais. All these young
people animated the quarter, giving it a gaiety and beauty
that could be sensed in the cafés, libraries and gardens as
well as in the lecture halls. After May, measures were taken
to prevent a repetition of such unwelcome events. First of
all, the streets were asphalted, to prevent the paving stones
being ripped up. Then students were dispersed to new fac-
ulties far from the centre, access to which could be easily
controlled. It is true of course that there was congestion, but
this could have been tackled differently.

Another development, rather later, was the dismantling of
the stronghold of publishing in the 6th arrondissement. To

recall, Hachette had its large building on the corner of the Boulevard Saint-Germain and the Boulevard Saint-Michel, Flammarion was on the Rue Racine, Robert Laffont on the Place Saint-Sulpice, Larousse on the Boulevard Raspail, Le Seuil on the Rue Jacob, Hazan on the Rue de Seine, Nathan on the Rue Monsieur-le-Prince – the list could be continued. But with the capitalist concentration of publishing, and the replacement of editors by accountants concerned with return on investments, many large houses abandoned their historic headquarters and moved out to glass and metal buildings near the Periphérique. A few major publishers have remained in the quarter, Gallimard, Minuit, Fayard and Bourgois among others, but they are like vestiges of a past splendour.

A few years earlier, contemporary art had already abandoned the Left Bank. In 1960, at the time of the 'new realists', galleries were concentrated in a quadrilateral bordered by the Rue Guénégaud, the Rue Bonaparte, the Boulevard Saint-Germain and the Seine. On the Right Bank there was hardly anything except antiques. By the 1990s, however, for reasons that no doubt had to do with rent levels, contemporary art migrated en masse, first to the Bastille quarter and then to the Marais. There are still a few fine galleries on the Left Bank, and many excellent shops selling 1960s furniture and African art, but once again, 'it's not like it was'.

Booksellers, too – another traditional activity of the Left Bank – are on the decline. Many small bookshops have closed, but above all, four major establishments have disappeared that were institutions and almost symbols of the Latin Quarter: François Maspero's La Joie de Lire on the Rue Saint-Séverin, which was the political university of a whole generation; Les Presses Universitaires de France on the Place de la Sorbonne, a major academic bookshop; then more recently the Moniteur on the Place de l'Odéon, irreplaceable for architecture; and finally La Hune, on the corner of the Place Saint-Germain-des-Près and the Rue Bonaparte. During my school years, a shop known as Le Divan was run there by an old-style author-publisher-bookseller, Henri Martineau, the great specialist in Stendhal of his time. He was kind enough to present me with copies of *Henry Brulard* and *Les Souvenirs d'égotisme*, in editions that were admirable both typographically and philologically. This corner has now reverted to luxury goods, like the former La Hune shop on the Boulevard Saint-Germain, which is today a Vuitton outlet, the very standard-bearer of bourgeois vulgarity.

These various changes have had convergent effects: 'intellectual life' has disappeared from the Left Bank. It is true that this is an unpleasant term that covered a great deal of snobbery and caste spirit, but something of the spirit of Sartre, Giacometti, Perec and Genet hovered in these streets, not to mention Mastroianni, a loyal customer of Le Balto, on the corner of the Rue Mazarine and the Rue Guénégaud. Luxury clothes and accessories have driven out their ghosts, and 'made all who are Parisians at heart tremble', as Louis-Sébastien Mercier wrote about a certain destruction on the Chaussée d'Antin.

I return now to the Rue Saint-Jacques after this long parenthesis that began on the Rue des Ursulines. Slipping between Saint-Jacques-du-Haut-Pas and the Institut des Sourds-Muets, I enter the Rue de l'Abbé-de-l'Épée (a good abbot, founder of this institute). It is bordered on the left by the long wall that encloses the institute's garden, and on the right by fancy buildings of which no. 14, dated 1909, is given a timid Art Nouveau stamp by its sculpted leaves, the curves of its balconies, and the ironwork volutes at its entry. I was born here in July 1936, and lived here for the next four years. The earliest memory I have is in this apartment:

14 *Rue de l'Abbé-de-l'Épée and the church of Saint-Jacques-du-Haut-Pas.*

a friend of my parents, in uniform, coming to kiss me in my bed – this was undoubtedly autumn 1939. Then in June 1940, my family piled into a black 11CV Citroën just like you see in all the films about this episode, and took the road for Marseille.

On the corner of the Rue de l'Abbé-de-l'Épée and the Boulevard Saint-Michel, a recumbent naked woman pays strange homage in stone to two pharmacists who discovered the therapeutic virtues of quinine, Pelletier and Caventou. Walking opposite the long façade of the École des Mines, I reach the corner of the Rue Royer-Collard. From the 1960s to about 1985, this place was not only the terminus of the 85 bus, which ran to the Saint-Ouen *mairie* by a winding and magnificent trajectory, but also the site of a bookshop called Autrement Dit. Run first of all by Italians, it passed into the orbit of Éditions de Minuit. In spring 1984, Éditions Hazan, of which I had just become director, published its first book of the new era, *Duchamp*, with text by Jean-Christophe Bailly and drawings by Roman Cieslewicz. It

47

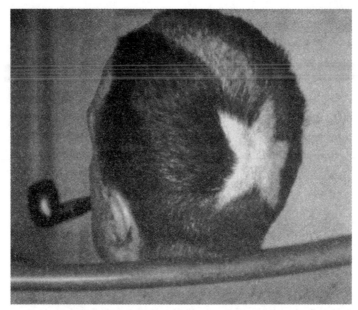

Roman Cieslewicz, cover image for Duchamp, Éditions Hazan, 1984.

was quite natural for us to choose Autrement Dit for the launch party, the unforgettable premiere to a long series of 'bookshop encounters', as they are called, which are one of the charms of the trade, the only moment when the publisher meets that multifarious and mysterious being, the reader.

A little later, when Éditions de Minuit won the Goncourt prize with Marguerite Duras's *The Lover*, the wise Jérôme Lindon, the very Nestor of publishing, bought with the money from the million copies sold, the Larousse offices opposite the Sorbonne and opened the fine bookshop Compagnie there. Autrement Dit was then closed, and its corner site is today occupied by a branch of Crédit Lyonnais.

CHAPTER 3

For a long while, I would make a detour in order to avoid the Luxembourg garden, too marked in my memory by Sunday afternoons when I was sent out to 'get some fresh air' – my mother had the hygienic ideas of her time. Once cured, I learned to love this garden, its two parts separated by a virtual line that follows the Paris meridian, across the fountain in the central pond and past the Senate clock. To the east, the Saint-Michel side, is the young Luxembourg: students and schoolchildren, young foreigners enjoying themselves, sandwiches on the benches and limbs bronzing in the first spring sun. To the west, the Montparnasse side, around the tennis courts, the children's play area and the beekeeping pavilion, is a calmer and less busy Luxembourg: bourgeois from the Rue Guynemer, psychoanalysts and foreign diplomats, swarthy nursemaids in charge of blond children. On this side, along a path with immense plane trees surrounded by water, Dalou's monument to Delacroix shows how, starting from an agreed programme (allegorical figures around a plinth supporting a bust), constraint can give rise to a masterpiece.

It was on a deserted path in the Luxembourg garden that Marius met Cosette and Jean Valjean for the first time, 'a man and a quite young girl sitting almost side by side on the same bench, at the most solitary end of the path, by the Rue de l'Ouest [now d'Assas]'. Nerval depicts a similar meeting in his *Odellete*, titled 'An Alley in the Luxembourg':

The girl passed,
Lively and swift as a bird:
In her hand a shining flower,
In her mouth a new tune.

Verlaine, Cendras, Rilke, Léautaud, Sartre, Faulkner, Eche-
noz... Few places in Paris have inspired so many writers and
poets, not to mention cineastes – Jean-Luc Godard's joyous
All the Boys are Named Patrick, or Louis Malle's darker
The Fire Within.

Emerging from the Luxembourg, I pass behind the Odéon
theatre. I believe there were still booksellers under these
arcades in the early postwar years, but nothing compara-
ble with the time when Courteline, Marcel Schwob, Catulle
Mendès or Barrès hung about here to see how their books
were selling, according to Léon Daudet in *Paris vécu*.[1]

The corner of Rue de Condé and Rue de Tournon is
broken off, creating a space badly filled by a little garden
and a newspaper kiosk. At one time this was the site of
Foyot, a famous restaurant, popular with the members
of the nearby Senate. In 1893, at the time of 'propaganda
of the deed', an anarchist bomb blew up the restaurant –
though this was hardly a success, as not only was no senator
present, but a sympathizer with their cause, Laurent Tailhade, happened to be dining there and lost an eye. Some
believe that the bomb was planted by Félix Fénéon himself,
the best critic of his time (so said Mallarmé), and later editorial secretary of *La Revue blanche*. This is by no means
certain, but Fénéon was among the accused in the famous
'trial of the Thirty' in August 1894: detonators had been
found in the office of the war ministry where he was chief
clerk. The charge here was 'association with malefactors',
but the *lois scélérates* of 1893, though making defence of
terrorism a criminal offence, had not provided for special

anti-terrorist courts, and the jury found all the defendants not guilty.

The Rue de Tournon is for me one of the loveliest in Paris, for the buildings it contains but above all for its bell shape, the way that its two sides diverge after the Rue Saint-Sulpice to frame the central pavilion of the Luxembourg palace in a proud scenic arrangement. This was in no way accidental. When the Comte de Provence, brother of Louis XVI and future Louis XVIII, divided up the land that he owned here, the men who designed this quarter in the 1780s paid the site great attention. Proof of this is the two opposing triangles, one with its point at the Odéon theatre and its sides on Rue Crébillion and Rue Casimir-Delavigne, the other with its point at the Odéon crossroads and its sides on Rue Monsieur-le-Prince and Rue de Condé. The common side of these triangles is Rue d'Odéon, the first street in Paris to have been bordered with sidewalks. The ensemble is drawn with a flexible asymmetry that tempers its rigour and makes walking a joy.

For the Luxembourg palace, the Florentine Marie de Médicis wanted a building inspired by the Palazzo Pitti. She entrusted its execution to Salomon de Brosse, who, as a good Protestant, had his own ideas. While reproducing formal details of the Florentine palace – the bosses and the ringed Tuscan columns – he built a French-style château. The central pavilion has a grace due largely to its imperfections, the hesitations perceptible in its details, its transgressions of the rules. Just as the awkwardness of adolescents may be more touching than full-blown beauty, so architectural gaucheness is often more attractive than classical constructions. The time when the Luxembourg was built, around 1610, was an uncertain period in architectural terms, when Gothic had not yet completely disappeared in Paris (the Gothic church of Saint-Eustache was completed under Louis XVIII), when the Renaissance still remained discrete, and the Baroque had not successfully established itself. Hence the imperfect and charming architecture of the façade of Saint-Gervais, by the same Salomon de Brosse, or the dome of Saint-Paul seen from the Rue Charlemagne.

In the Rue de Tournon, several plaques remind us of illustrious former residents. One plaque, above the Café Tournon, informs us of the final years spent there by Joseph Roth, who drowned the chagrin of exile in alcohol. The two sides of the street are symmetrical in line, but different in physiognomy. On the right, as you go downhill, you have a homogeneous set of buildings from the late eighteenth and early nineteenth centuries, with the majority of shops now devoted to luxury clothing. The left side is a succession of noble neoclassical *hôtels*. One of these, at no. 10, was transformed into a barracks and served as a major slaughterhouse for prisoners during the June Days of 1848. Leibniz stayed in an annex to this *hôtel* when he lived in Paris in the 1670s and invented the infinitesimal calculus.

A dog's-leg via the Rue Saint-Sulpice leads to the start of the Rue de l'Odéon, where nothing, no plaque or souvenir, recalls that these few metres were a great centre of world literature in the interwar years. At no. 7, Adrienne Monnier opened a lending library in 1915 under the sign La Maison des Amis des Livres. Almost opposite, at no. 12, her partner Sylvia Beach founded a bookshop on the same principles in 1921, Shakespeare and Company.[2] The list of women and men who frequented these enchanted premises is too long to be given completely here. We may just mention, for Adrienne Monnier's shop, André Gide and Paul Valéry, Henri Michaux, Aragon, Michel Leiris, Valéry Larbaud, Léon-Paul Fargue, Saint-John Perse, Walter Benjamin, Italo Svevo... While on the other side, at Sylvia Beach's, you could come across Gertrude Stein, F. Scott Fitzgerald, Ernest

Hemingway, Djuna Barnes, Ezra Pound or James Joyce, whose *Ulysses* Sylvia published in 1922, at a time when the book had been banned in the United States, Great Britain and Ireland. This short stretch of street bears the memory of an unexampled adventure in literary history, and all book-lovers should make a little mental salute when they pass by.

To find the Paris of the Great Revolution in today's city takes a good deal of imagination. The most famous sites have been destroyed, and the most glorious names are largely absent. The noisy Odéon crossroads, for example, offers only few vestiges to remind us that it was the main centre of the Revolution on the Left Bank.

The topography here was greatly transformed by the cutting of the Boulevard Saint-Germain. At the time of the Revolution, a narrow roadway, Rue des Boucheries, closely followed the line of the present boulevard before continuing directly via the Rue de l'École-de-Médicine. The Cour du Commerce, today amputated by the boulevard, was much longer, extending from the Rue Saint-André-des-Arts as far as the Rue de l'École-de-Médicine.

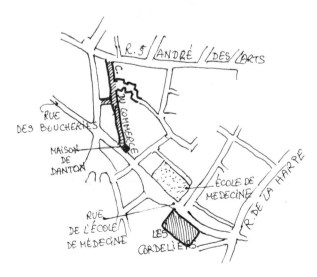

Just as the Société des Amis de la Constitution took its name from its premises in the Jacobins monastery, so the Société des Amis des Droits de l'Homme et du Citoyen became the Cordeliers club once it had settled in the monastery of that order, almost opposite the colonnade of the École de Médicine. But the symmetry stops there. At the Cordeliers, recruitment, attendance and operation were more plebeian than at the Jacobins. The entrance fee was symbolic, anyone wishing to join could do so, women were allowed to speak, and the main orators were neither advocates nor any kind of lawyer, but laymen who came from the theatre (Hébert), printing (Momoro) or medicine (Chaumette). Danton often came to the Cordeliers, but the club's hero was Marat. After his assassination, his heart, placed in an urn, was suspended from the ceiling of the meeting room at a solemn ceremony.

The Cordeliers are rather poorly viewed by historians of all stripes: vulgar bawlers with no clear political vision, always ready for untimely insurrections. Yet they were the first to demand the dismissal of the king after the flight to Varennes, to organize the revolution of 10 August 1792 that put an end to the monarchy, and to launch the great campaign of de-Christianization in the autumn of year II, which saw all Paris churches closed for worship. This was where the sans-culottes of the faubourgs and popular quarters came to discuss and debate. The only writer to do them justice was Gustave Tridon, Blanqui's right arm:

> Hail to you, Hébert and Pache, pure and noble citizens; Chaumette, whom the people loved as a father; Momoro, an ardent pen and generous spirit; Ronsin, intrepid general; and you, Anacharsis Cloots – gentle and melancholy figure through whom German pantheism linked hands with French naturalism! Pride and ambition concealed by

hypocritical formulas sacrificed these men, and the Revolution perished with them.[3]

The Cour du Commerce was also an important site in the years of Revolution, but today it is so densely packed with eateries as to inhibit the imagination. This was not yet the case when I started publishing in the 1980s; the trade counter of Éditions du Seuil was at no. 4. A prominent position was occupied by a tower from the wall of Philippe Auguste, today submerged in an immense patisserie occupying nos. 4, 6 and 8, where Marat established his printing press in 1793 after several more temporary premises. Opposite at no. 9, Dr Guillotin perfected his celebrated machine in the workshop of a carpenter, and is said to have experimented with it on sheep.

Danton lived in a large building at no. 20 on the Cour du Commerce, in the section now displaced by the Boulevard Saint-Germain. This was just where his statue now stands, which is rather exceptional. How is it that Danton has a monument, a street and cafés that bear his name, while Robespierre has nothing in Paris that evokes his memory? After all, it was Danton who established the revolutionary tribunal, Danton who said: 'They want to terrorize us, let us be terrible!' But at the start of the Third Republic it was he whom the Radicals chose as an emblematic figure, doubtless more presentable to their eyes than Robespierre.

The Cour de Rohan opens off the Cour du Commerce, a succession of three small courtyards, calm and aristocratic, where Virginia creepers and climbing roses festoon seventeenth-century buildings. In this haven protected by money, often the only people you meet are a few students from the Lycée Fénelon with their sandwiches.

Through the Rue du Jardinet and the Rue Serpente, I enter one of the oldest streets on the Left Bank, the Rue

Turret, Rue Hautefeuille.

© Cléo Marelli

Hautefeuille, where Baudelaire was born and where Cour-bet had his studio. On the corner of a small cul-de-sac, a bartizan or hanging turret dating from the sixteenth century ornaments the *hôtel* of the abbots of Fécamp. Its conical trunk is made of a knotwork series in decreasing diame-ter, each ring bearing a different decoration – a masterpiece of masonry. There are few bartizans left in Paris. On the Left Bank there is another on the same Rue Hautefeuille, on a fine *hôtel* between the Rue Pierre-Sarrazin and the Rue de l'École-de-Médicine. On the Right Bank, if I am not mistaken, they are all in the Marais: a square one, almost rustic, on the corner of Rue Sainte-Croix-de-la-Bretonnerie and Rue du Temple; one on the corner of Rue Saint-Paul and Rue des Lions-Saint-Paul (there used to be lions in the great menagerie of the Hôtel Saint-Pol, a royal residence under the Valois); another on the flamboyant Gothic turret of the Hôtel Hérouet, on the corner of Rue Vieille-du-Temple and Rue des Quatre-Fils; one on the turrets that

56

frame the gateway of the Hôtel de Clisson on the Rue des Archives, and that of the Hôtel de Sens on the Rue du Figuier; and finally, at the corner of Rue Pavée and Rue des Francs-Bourgeois, one that decorates the corner of the Hôtel Lamoignon, one of the few Renaissance buildings in Paris. All these are friends of mine, some on habitual routes, others that I make a little detour in order to greet. Each person has their punctuation marks in the city.

The most remarkable thing on the Place Saint-André-des-Arts is not the most apparent. 1 rue Danton could pass as one of the Art Nouveau 'lite' buildings that are so common in Paris. Yet this was exceptionally innovative in its time, even serving as a show building for its constructor, François Hennebique. At first sight, you would think it made of stone, but it is built entirely in concrete, including all of its sculptures and cornices. Around 1900, the Hennebique company constructed light and elegant buildings across the world, all in reinforced concrete.

By both day and night, the ensemble formed by Place Saint-André-des-Arts and Place Saint-Michel is lively and noisy, peopled with tourists, students and often also black and Arab youth, which is not so common on the Left Bank, where the Malians are mainly on building sites and the Algerians in delivery vehicles. The Saint-Michel fountain is the meeting point, where the archangel flooring the dragon symbolizes, in Dolf Oehler's words, 'the victory of the imperial and bourgeois order over the revolution, the triumph of Good over the bad people of June 1848'.[4]

The buildings arranged around the Place Saint-Michel are another representation of 'the imperial and bourgeois order'. With their high mezzanine arcades, their colossal pilasters, their balustrade balconies, they are examples of a monumental and almost neoclassical version of Haussmannism. To the east side you have the Rue de la Huchette and the Rue Saint-Séverin, linked for me and many others with the memory of La Joie de Lire. As this bookshop used to remain open very late, I would go there in the evenings after work. You met friends there, discussed with strangers and joked with the booksellers, pretty girls who liked to guess what book each entering customer would buy. And you sometimes saw, silently passing, the thin and elegant figure of François Maspero, whom I never dared speak to at that time.

It was thanks to Éditions Maspero and La Joie de Lire that I made the acquaintance of Frantz Fanon, Louis Althusser, Paul Nizan, Jean-Pierre Vernant, Fernand Deligny, John Reed, Alexandra Kollontai, Rosa Luxemburg – later than others did, but the surgeon's trade sadly demands a certain narrowness of focus. Maspero books were magnificent in their typography, their colours, the quality of their paper and printing. I had dozens of them, since lost in successive moves, or lent and not returned, but that is no serious matter – they existed and they nourished me. I buy them again when I find them.

Fined, confiscated, bombed – neither the publishing house nor the Maspero bookshop ever gave in. There is only one other house whose courage and inventiveness could stand comparison: Éditions de Minuit. The others are old maids. Maspero and Jérôme Lindon are heroes from the days of my youth. A street has been named after Gaston Gallimard. Saint Séverin would not complain if one day half of his street was renamed after François Maspero.

To reach the Châtelet from the Place Saint-Michel, the simplest route would be to go straight ahead, but that would force me to walk between the Palais de Justice, the Préfecture de Police and the Tribunal de Commerce – a sorry prospect. A dog's-leg via the Petit-Pont would involve crossing the queue of tourists in front of Notre-Dame and then walking between the bare wall of the Hôtel-Dieu and the T-shirt stands of the Rue d'Arcole, which is hardly more attractive. In other words, there is no pleasant trajectory to cross the middle of the Île de la Cité.

After the victory of the coming revolution, the sequels of Haussmann's town-planning assault on this place will have to be cleared. I would happily propose destroying the Hôtel-Dieu and the Préfecture de Police, which would liberate a great space between the two arms of the Seine, from the Palais de Justice (to be transformed into rehearsal and concert halls) to the façade of Notre-Dame. The dismantled stones would be carefully preserved, as building workers from Seine-Saint-Denis would then be entrusted with constructing housing and community facilities on this site. Wouldn't that be a great idea? Some might fear a shantytown, but I rather think that people would come from across the world to admire this marvel of a new style. It would be the start of a reconquest of Paris.

In the meantime, my choice is to cross the Seine by the Pont-Neuf. To avoid the chaos of the Quai des Grands-Augustins and the kebab joints of the Rue Saint-André-des-Arts, I can zigzag between the two. (On the *quai*, at least, I have a friendly stopover, L'Écluse, today a restaurant offering a fine selection of Bordeaux wines, but which was in the 1950s a cabaret where I heard for the first time Georges Brassens, and later Barbara.)

The Rue de l'Hirondelle, which starts beneath an arcade on the Place Saint-Michel, is today almost deserted. Francis Carco tells that before the First World War this was the site of La Bolée, a replica of the Lapin Agile in the Latin Quarter, where 'the clientele, made up of anarchists, prowlers, students, singers, comics, errand girls and poor wretches, feasted cheaply, not at all like a first-class waiting room but rather a third-class one, among dirty wrapping paper, charcuterie and pitchers of cider'.[5] There is no longer any trace of the time when the Latin Quarter was dirty and wretched, and the surroundings of the Collège de France the domain of rag-pickers. During the first half of the twentieth century the quarter was gradually disinfected, and the landscape of the 1920s that Léautaud describes in his *Journal*, Daudet in *Paris vécu* and Gide in *The Counterfeiters* was already very different from that of Carco.

With hardly any traffic, and neither shops nor cafés, the Rues Gît-le-Coeur, Séguier and de Savoie are white, calm and silent at any time of day or year. It is not easy to know who lives here, as you do not meet many people. The Rue des Grands-Augustins is more lively (before the Revolution, the Grands-Augustins was an immense monastery on the bank of the Seine, between the Tour de Nesle and the street that today bears its name; the Rue Dauphine was cut through its gardens). At no. 7, a plaque indicates that Picasso painted *Guernica* here, and that this was where Balzac located the action of *The Unknown Masterpiece*.

The crossroads where the Rue du Pont-de-Lodi comes out into the Rue Dauphine almost opposite the Rue de Nesle is the domain of the cut-price book dealers. This activity is both discrete and considerable: thousands of volumes leave here for the bargain bookshops that can be found all across France. When I started in publishing, I knew four of the five characters who reigned over this place. By dint of seeing whole swathes of publishers come here over the years, they came to possess a predictive skill, an acute sense of what makes for the success or failure of a book. For the neophyte that I was, this was a precious experience, which often enabled me to jettison doubtful projects. One of their number, René Beaudoin, founded the shop Mona Lisait, where you could find in the basement rare titles that he had republished himself. A great cyclist – he trained the youth team at Gennevilliers – he was run over and killed by a lorry on the Quai de la Mégisserie. The others are still there with their wide range of books behind dark windows that in no way attract the attention of the passer-by.

Looking back from the Pont-Neuf, you see the Monnaie, the Institut de France, the corner of the Louvre colonnade and the Apollo gallery, the clock-tower and nave of Saint-Germain-l'Auxerrois, the top of the Saint-Jacques tower and the façade of Saint-Gervais, the towers of the Palais de Justice, and, on the bridge itself, the two twin buildings that frame the entrance to the Place Dauphine. In this panorama I read a kind of unity that is not simply due to habit: these buildings were all constructed in Paris stone (Louis-Sébastien Mercier: 'These towers, these belfries, these vaults of temples, so many signs that say to the eye: what you see in the air is missing beneath our feet'[6]). And the common origin of their material gives this diverse range of monuments a common tint, with subtle variations of Parisian grey. All attest to the great art of successive generations of stonemasons.

This landscape, it is true, is now no more than a vast museum. The dog trainers, lightermen and water-carriers who once animated it have long since disappeared, but after all one has a right to be happy in a museum, as indeed a few steps away regarding the lances of Paolo Uccello or Nicolas Poussin's *Rebecca*, so gracious in her blue dress by the fountain.

The ensemble formed by the Pont-Neuf, the Place Dauphine and the Rue Dauphine was the first case of concerted improvement in Paris. ('Dauphine' in honour of the little Dauphin, the future Louis XIII, born in 1601.) Henri IV launched two other major projects: the Place Royale (now Place de Vosges), which became so much the centre of elegant life in Paris that people simply said 'the *place*'; and the Place de France, which was left on the drawing board after Henri's assassination. This was to be a semi-circle in the Temple marshes, the intended seat of the royal administration. Its diameter would have been along the city wall (on the Boulevard des Filles-du-Calvaire, near the Cirque d'Hiver), and from its centre would have radiated streets bearing the names of French provinces. The names still remain in this quarter: Poitou, Normandie, Franche-Comté, Beauce... That the plans for the Place Dauphine, the Place Royale and the Place de France were drawn according to the three basic geometrical figures, triangle, square and circle, shows that nothing was left to chance in this project of urban improvement.[7]

The Place Dauphine has undergone a series of assaults that have done it a good deal of harm. Under the Third Republic, the construction of the massive west façade of the Palais de Justice meant the destruction of the base of the triangle, though for André Breton, when he wrote *Nadja* in the 1920s, this was still 'one of the most remote places', 'one of the worst wastelands' of Paris. Then, around 1970, an underground car park was dug beneath the place, ravaging it like the Place Vendôme, Place Saint-Sulpice and many others have been. The ground was raised, and the old cobbles replaced by a sandy covering for scrawny chestnut trees. The result seems to be a public garden that they have not ventured to name as such. Finally, from the 1990s, restaurants mushroomed up along two sides of the triangle, quite taking away its charm. Chez Paul, where I sometimes used to invite my medical students (the young ones at the bottom of the hospital hierarchy), still exists, but now lacks the ambiance of an old Parisian bistrot with its check tablecloths, surly waiters, leeks in vinegar and *blanquette de veau*.

The narrow Rue du Roule runs past the Samaritaine department store, named after a pavilion on piles that was moored to the Pont-Neuf, with a pump and a chiming clock. Mercier notes that 'this clock face, seen and questioned by so many passers-by, has gone for months without telling the time. The chimes are as defective as the clock itself; they publicly spout nonsense, but at least people are entitled to make fun of them.'[8] The great Samaritaine store, for its part, closed its doors some ten years ago, on the pretext of security – a blatant pretext, but since the owner (Bernard Arnault, LVMH) is a major advertising client, the press showed more than its usual prudence on this occasion.

We are right to be concerned about the future of Frantz Jourdain and Henri Sauvage's masterwork, even if the project has been entrusted to the Japanese agency SANAA, one of the most highly regarded at the moment, whose buildings in France include the Louvre-Lens. The plans envisage shopping galleries in the basement, ground and first floor, above them office space to finance the project, and on top a luxury hotel – eighty suites with a view of the Seine. We must wish the architects good luck, as the building is highly listed and thus impossible to 'façade' – in other words, to gut like a chicken and just keep the shell. The stairs, banisters, the whole precious Art Deco ironwork have to be preserved, and it will not be easy to make the new floors coincide with those of the original building. So as not to ruffle the sensitivity of the Paris municipality, always sharp-eyed as we know, permission to modify the town-planning regulations and build higher has been obtained by including social housing and a crèche. In short, while the choice of architects will probably make it possible to avoid disaster, money and luxury will certainly deprive the good people of one of their traditional haunts for browsing and buying, a store in which 'you could find anything', climbed by King Kong in a famous advertisement of the 1970s. The Samaritaine terrace, with its viewpoint indicator and its 360-degree view over the roofs of Paris, will remain accessible to the public, but only in groups of twelve escorted by two fire-fighters.⁹ It is true that in the meantime LVMH will have offered Parisians the Vuitton foundation in the Bois de Bou-logne – a building conceived by Frank Gehry, the architect most prominent in the global media, for Bernard Arnault, the richest man in France.

From the Rue du Roule, I can see the rose window of the transept of Saint-Eustache. In *October Nights*, Nerval wanders into the Halles with a friend:

> This magnificent structure, which blends the flamboyance of the Middle Ages with the more severe symmetries of the Renaissance, is beautifully illuminated by the moonlight, which plays on its Gothic armature, its flying buttresses which protrude like the ribs of some prodigious whale and the Roman arches of its windows and doors, whose ornaments seem to belong to its ogival section.

As the two night-time walkers advance,

> The floor of Les Halles was beginning to stir to life. The carts of the various wholesale merchants of dairy prod-ucts, fish, produce and vegetables were arriving in an uninterrupted stream. The carters who had finished their haul were having drinks in the various nearby all-night cafés and taverns. On the Rue Mauconseil, these estab-lishments stretch all the way to the oyster market; they line the Rue Montmartre from the edge of Saint-Eustache to the Rue du Jour. On the right side of this street you find the eel-mongers; the left side is occupied by the Raspail pharmacies and by licensed cider houses – where you can also get yourself excellent oysters and tripe à la mode de Caen ... As we made our way to the left of the fish

market, where things only begin to liven up around five or six in the morning when the bidding starts, we noticed a bunch of men sprawled on sacks of green beans, wearing smocks, berets and white jackets with black stripes . . . Some of them were keeping warm like soldiers huddled around their campfires, others were sitting around their portable stoves in the nearby taverns. Still others were standing near the piles of sacks, discussing the price of beans, using such terms as options, extensions, profit margins, consignments, selling up, selling short – as if they were playing the stock market.[10]

This is clearly Les Halles before Baltard, but what Nerval describes is not too different from the atmosphere I remember from the 1960s, when I came shopping with the Necker hospital cook to prepare for a feast in the staff room. (This was where the interns slept and ate.) The women and men who worked in Les Halles were still like the legends told of them from François Villon to Jean-Pierre Melville. In their clothing, their speech, their very gestures, they had (especially the women) a style, an inventiveness, a humour, a cordiality, that you still find a trace of in certain Paris markets – formerly at the Enfants-Rouges, today at Aligre. Those not old enough to have known Les Halles before their destruction can at least study the photographs that Robert Doisneau took of them over many years: the thousands of crates, the caps, the faces, the overalls, the mist on café windows, the fish and the hams, the flowers and the onions, the lorries, the lights... All that is missing is the smells and the noises. A little further on, the Beaubourg plateau, flat as its name implies and covered with large paving stones, was the lorry park.

In *L'Assassinat de Paris*, Louis Chevalier recalls the reasons given by those who planned to destroy Les Halles in

Robert Doisneau, Les Halles.

the late 1950s.[11] The main argument was the traffic jams, one of the great complaints of the time – Pompidou's project was to adapt Paris to the automobile, and the destruction of Les Halles would be the centrepiece of this adaptation.

> [Traffic jams] which the interested parties, the lorry-drivers, navigated marvellously, and which they would have been the last to complain about. And the traffic jams throughout the city, and increasingly throughout the conurbation, which the market traffic is held responsible for, although in the early hours of the morning, on an empty and newly washed Boulevard Sébastopol, you can drive very easily, which paradoxically ceases to be the case after Les Halles have closed.

Then there was hygiene:

the legendary dirtiness of Les Halles. Goods left in the open air in every season, exposed to heat, cold, rain, sun, in the dust and mud of the pavements, on the roadway, in the gutter, over drains. It will be understood that I am quoting wholesale the words that I find in this discourse without attempting to put them in order, to arrange them in the way that goods, vegetables for example, are arranged in harmonious constructions that, in the bright light of the lamps, breathe order, beauty, taste and quite obviously cleanliness: so fresh and neat that it would be a shame even to peel them . . . Curiously, the hygiene argument, brandished by the opponents of Les Halles and the champions of a 'definitive solution', was one of the arguments of those shameless people who had the effrontery to defend the destruction of the old port of Marseille: also a miraculous quarter, so like that of Les Halles in many ways, by its fate, by the striking memory that it left right across the world, and above all by the charges made against it, one of these being the danger to public health: enough to make a whale laugh.

To dramatize things yet more, there were the rats, 'the old medieval fear of rats. "An army of rats", the word "army" making the danger all the more striking. Despite not having heard the workers at Les Halles talking of their encounters with rats, it made the listeners' flesh creep, like the fisherman's famous tale about the octopus.' And to complete the spectacle, 'Villon's fat prostitutes, very far from discreet, some of whom displayed their charms even on the steps of Saint-Eustache'.

Louis Chevalier, who taught the history of Paris at the Collège de France, had been a fellow student of Georges Pompidou at the École Normale Supérieure, and they continued to lunch together from time to time in a small restaurant on the Rue Hautefeuille.

We spoke about everything, our youth, our teachers, our classmates, life, love, poetry, never about philosophy, which neither of us took to, and of course, absolutely never about politics. Also, coming to the point, never about Paris. And yet God knows that on some days the subject imposed itself, burning to be served hot on a plate in the middle of the table. For example, the day after a certain declaration about the Place de la Défense and its towers, published in *Le Monde*. At the very moment I sat down at the table, it still sat uneasily on my stomach. It seemed to me – perhaps just an illusion – that Pompidou, knowing my ideas on the question were exactly the opposite of his, cast me a smug and inflexible look, which probably meant that with people like me, the people of Paris would still dwell in the huts where Caesar found them.

May '68 certainly played in favour of the fatal decision. Not that anything much happened at Les Halles during the 'events', but the physical and moral clean-up of the capital was in the spirit of the time. Finally, on 27 February 1969, Les Halles were moved out to Rungis.

Should Baltard's pavilions have been kept? I am unsure. Between the move and their destruction in 1971–2, they were indeed spaces for theatre, dance and music, open for all kinds of events that had no official status, but representing on the contrary a way of defying the authorities and continuing the spirit of May. Had they been given over to commerce and culture, it is likely that they would have experienced the fate of other places preserved after the end of their original activity, sad 'spaces' devoted to the sale of T-shirts and souvenirs, to fast food or museums in exile: Covent Garden in London, the Liverpool docks, the Fiat Lingotto in Turin, the port of San Francisco.

But what happened in the 1970s between Saint-Eustache, the Rue Saint-Honoré, the Bourse de Commerce and the Boulevard Sébastopol is truly flabbergasting. In 1974, Giscard became president. This gave him control of Les Halles, along with the prefect of the Seine department, as Paris had not had a mayor since the time of the Revolution and was under the close control of the executive. The Gaullists on the municipal council were sidelined, and the renovation of Les Halles entrusted to a young Catalan architect, Ricardo Bofill. After his project of a great colonnade in Bernini style was rejected, he proposed a more acceptable plan, and his first buildings, more Haussmannian, began to rise from the ground, while the famous hole was dug that was to serve for the Métro station and the future RER.

Everything changed when Chirac became mayor of Paris in 1977. He declared, in a brash rejection of Giscard's pretentiousness: 'I shall be the architect in chief of Les Halles, without hang-ups . . . I want it to smell of chips!'[12] Bofill was dismissed (as compensation he was given the renovation of the Vercingétorix quarter), and his buildings, some of which were already three storeys high, were demolished. In the end, the plans adopted were those of Claude Vasconi, and, for the gardens, those of Louis Arretche, known for French-style fine art.

There remained the question of the hole. The digging had to be very deep in order to put the RER station at the same level as the Paris Métro, and the excavation was enormous – to get an idea of this, it is worth seeing *Touche pas la femme blanche*, an excellent parody Western shot inside the hole by Marco Ferreri, with Marcello Mastroianni and Catherine Deneuve. The station only occupied the bottom of the excavation. What should be done with the rest? After dismissing a number of far-fetched projects (such as a 'delphinarium' for dolphins and other cetaceans), the joint public-private

Touche pas la femme blanche, *film by Marco Ferreri. Collection Christophel.*

company in charge of the operation (SEMAH), concerned for its profitability, decided to give the biggest slice of the cake to the commercial centre that we know today under the name of the Forum. Since that time, the people who decide on the future of Les Halles are the powerful association representing the businesses established there and the developer Espace Expansion, a branch of Unibail. The hundreds of thousands of Parisians and *banlieusards* who pass through every morning remain underground, well protected from air and light.[13]

At the time that I visited Les Halles to take notes, the construction of the new 'canopy' was still unfinished. As Wittgenstein advises, 'whereof we cannot speak, thereof we must remain silent'.

The square defined by Rue des Innocents, Rue Saint-Denis and Rue Berger (the fourth side has neither form nor name) more or less corresponds to the space occupied until the end of the eighteenth century by the Innocents cemetery.

Jean Goujon's decorated fountain was not in the middle, as this was where the great pit was located that had received dozens of corpses every day since Philippe le Bel. It abutted the Innocents church, on the corner of Rue Saint-Denis and Rue aux Fers (now Berger), and so had only three sides. The cemetery was decorated with *danses macabres* such as were frequently painted in the fifteenth century, and we are told by Sauval – a historian of Paris who wrote in the 1650s – of a most marvellous skeleton by Germain Pilon. Jean Goujon, Germain Pilon: if French painting lagged somewhat behind in the fifteenth century, sculpture was at a peak. Those who prefer to see statues in their place of origin may admire in the church of Saint-Paul Germain Pilon's *Vierge de douleur*, and by Jean Goujon, besides the adorable nymphs on the Fontaine des Innocents, *Les Quatre Saisons* in the court of the Carnavelet museum.

The Innocents was no ordinary cemetery. Beneath the arches along its walls (the mass graves where bones were piled up to relieve the overcrowded pits), all kinds of ambulant pedlars, from linen maids to fortune-tellers, made it a centre of Parisian life. It was also one of the only three places illuminated in the deep night of medieval Paris, the two others being the Porte du Grand-Châtelet and the Tour de Nesle, where a lantern signalled to mariners navigating the Seine that they were reaching the city.

Towards the end of the Ancien Régime, however, a new concern for hygiene arose. 'The knowledge recently acquired on the nature of air cast a very clear light on the danger of this pollution', wrote Mercier. The result was that in 1780 the cemetery was closed, and the bones transferred to the quarries south of Paris that were henceforth known as the Catacombes. What a removal! 'Just imagine the flaming torches, this immense pit open for the first time, the fires fuelled with coffin planks, this frightening enclosure suddenly lit up in the silence of night!'[14] The church and the mass graves were then demolished, and the ground paved to serve as a marketplace. The fountain was dismantled and rebuilt stone by stone in the centre, but a fourth side was now needed. The task was entrusted to Pajou, a neoclassical sculptor, who acquitted himself honourably – this is today the south-facing side.

The narrow portion of the Rue Saint-Denis that leads to Châtelet crosses or adjoins streets heavy with history. To the right, along the arcades of the Rue de la Ferronnerie, Henri IV was killed with a dagger by Ravaillac while on his way to inaugurate the chapel of the Saint-Louis hospital. To the left, the Rue de La Reynie bears the name of the first lieutenant-general of police, appointed by Colbert in 1667, who set out to suppress seditious writings, close the Courts of Miracles, and expel what remained of the poor and deviant after the '*grande refermement*' of 1657, when the homeless population – beggars, mad, vagabonds, prostitutes – were collected and locked up in the Salpêtrière or Bicêtre. La Reynie was also responsible for the first public lighting, glass cages containing candles that were hung on ropes outside the first floor of buildings. Further on, the Rue des Lombards evokes the memory of the Italian money-changers and money-lenders established there from the time of Philippe Auguste.

Along the way, I ponder the fact that I am recounting this walk as if it were done at one go, as if I had completed the trajectory in a single day, without stopping for a coffee or to shelter from the rain, without ever breaking it off to resume the next day. And so there is a share of fiction and even improbability in the account. For justification, I can cite an illustrious precedent, that of Proust's *Time Regained*. Alone in the library of the Prince de Guermantes, the narrator explains that after so many years wasted in idleness and indecision, he is going to get to work and finally write a book . . . the book that we have just read in three thousand pages. Nor is this the only affront to verisimilitude in this final volume of Proust's magnum opus. Combray, which had previously been situated in the Beauce, in 1916 suddenly becomes a village on the front line of the war, somewhere in Champagne. 'The battle of Méséglise', Gilberte writes to the narrator, 'lasted for more than eight months; the Germans lost in it more than six hundred thousand men, they destroyed Méséglise, but they did not capture it.'[15] This is not just one of those inconsequential trivialities scattered throughout the work, where a secondary character mentioned early on becomes a thousand pages later the cousin of someone else instead of being their nephew. Combray is a central place in the book, and its shift in location can only have been intentional. Similarly, after a long night-time walk with Charlus, 'descending the boulevards', the narrator leaves him, continues alone and happens to enter, to quench his thirst, what he believes to be a hotel but is in fact a brothel kept by Jupien, where Charlus has himself chained to the bedstead and whipped – a long passage, closely worked and deliberately improbable. Thus, the end of *Time Regained* becomes a night-time fairyland ('the ancient East of the *Thousand and One Nights* that I used to love so much'), lit by searchlights seeking the skies for German planes.

CHAPTER 4

Return to earth: Place du Châtelet, the geographic centre of present-day Paris. One might almost believe it has always been here, at the intersection of the north-south and east-west axes, yet it is purely a creation of Haussmann. At the time when Nerval, Balzac, Eugène Sue and the young Victor Hugo were writing, the quarter between the Hôtel de Ville and the Louvre colonnade was a tangle of medieval alleys, the densest in the whole city. At the start of *A Second Home*, Balzac describes the Rue du Tourniquet-Saint-Jean, 'formerly one of the most tortuous and gloomy streets in the old quarter that surrounds the Hôtel de Ville'. Even at its widest part it was no more than six feet across, and 'in rainy weather the gutter water was soon deep at the foot of the old houses, sweeping down with it the dust and refuse deposited at the corner-stones by the residents'.

As the dustcarts could not pass through, the inhabitants trusted to storms to wash their always miry alley; for how could it be clean? When the summer sun shed its perpendicular rays on Paris like a sheet of gold, but as piercing as the point of a sword, it lighted up the blackness of this street for a few minutes without drying the permanent damp that rose from the ground-floor to the first storey of these dark and silent tenements. The residents, who lighted their lamps at five o'clock in the month of June, in winter never put them out. To this day the enterprising wayfarer who should approach the Marais along the quays, past the end of the Rue du Chaume, the Rues de l'Homme Armé, des Billettes and des Deux-Portes, all leading to the Rue du Tourniquet, might think he had passed through cellars all the way.

All that remains of this are a few street names, Rue de la Tâcherie, Rue de la Coutellerie, Rue de la Verrerie. The Rue de la Vieille-Laterne, which Nerval chose to die in, ran from the Rue de la Vieille-Place-aux-Veaux to the Place du Châtelet of the time, and it is said that the spot where he hanged himself corresponds to the centre of the curtain of the Théâtre de la Ville. At that time, the Place du Châtelet was quite small, centred on the Victoire column built under the Empire. This was further east than the centre of the square designed by Haussmann, so that when he reconfigured the quarter, the column had to be shifted some ten metres further west.

Of the four sides of today's Châtelet, there are three that fulfil their role very well. To the south, the Seine and the view of the towers of the Palais de Justice; to the east and

The moving of Châtelet column.

west, the two theatres built by Davioud, almost symmetrical but not quite, with an eclecticism that is correct without being boring. It is the fourth side that doesn't work, making the Place du Châtelet a great traffic intersection rather than a place for strolling and meeting people. The Haussmann cuttings – Rue des Halles, Boulevard Sébastopol and the unfortunate Avenue Victoria – open gaps that the thin façade of the Chambre des Notaires fails to fill. As for the central reservation, walled off by an almost continuous metal balustrade, this is neglected indeed: a newspaper kiosk, a Métro entrance, a taxi rank, a cylindrical advertising column, some lines of sickly trees. Only the coping of the fountain around the column offers tourists anything to sit on, and in hot weather the sphinxes that spout water bring some freshness amid the heavy traffic.

The axis of the Boulevards Sébastopol and Strasbourg is a paradigm of Haussmann's cuttings, and a successful one, integrated both into language ('le Sébasto') and into the quarters that it runs through and connects. The extremities of the perspective are marked by the dome of the Tribunal de Commerce to the south and the glass panels of the Gare de l'Est to the north – François Loyer noted that this dome, oddly off-centre on a flat roof, has no function other than a visual one.[1] The great merit of this Haussmann cutting is that it did not destroy the quarters it opened up, except for the short section between Châtelet and the Rue de Rivoli, devastated as we have just seen. True, the boulevard did involve destruction, but this was limited in width. Neither the Rue Saint-Martin, nor the Rue Saint-Denis, nor the many small side streets, suffered significant damage; they keep the same lines and almost the same buildings as at the time of Balzac and the young Baudelaire.

Not all of Haussmann's grand projects show the same design. Some were tantamount to murder in the name of town-planning: wholesale clearing, massive and systematic destruction, displacement of population. These ravages particularly affected two zones towards which the Second Empire felt a mixture of fear and contempt: the Île de la Cité and the Hôtel de Ville quarter on the one hand, and then the region around the Place du Château-d'Eau, which would become the Place de la République.

In his *Mémoires*, Haussmann expresses his disgust for the vile crowd he was forced to pass through in walking from the Chausée-d'Antin where he lived to the law faculty where he was a student. The brigands, prostitutes and immigrant workers crowded into the sordid streets around the Hôtel de Ville and Notre-Dame had to be got rid of, being the source of both cholera and unpredictable riots. (These immigrant workers, who hailed from the Creuse – where there is still a village called Peintaparis – Corrèze or Brittany were viewed as Poles, Italians, Portuguese, Algerians and Malians would be later on.)

The second region marked for destruction, around the Château-d'Eau, was, along with the Faubourg Saint-Antoine, the most turbulent in the city, the quickest to erect barricades and fight to the death. In June 1848 – still a recent memory in Haussmann's time – it had taken tens of thousands of soldiers, supported by artillery, to supress the insurrection in the Faubourg du Temple. There was therefore no remedy short of wholesale clearance: an enormous hole was cut in the urban fabric, erasing the end of the Boulevard du Temple (the 'Boulevard du Crime' with all its theatres) and the start of the Boulevard Saint-Martin. This hole was transformed one way or another into a square whose essential element was the barracks – which still exists. From here, by new roadways (Rue Turbigo, Boulevard Magenta, the Canal Saint-Martin newly covered to make the Boulevard Richard-Lenoir), the cavalry and artillery could set out to every corner of the city. The difficulties subsequently experienced in improving the Place de la République were bound up with this past, as there is a difference in kind between an empty space to be bordered and a space expressly designed as a square.

But it was impossible to remove all the dangerous classes from Paris. Workers were need for the gigantic constructions that would turn the city upside down. Hence the second kind of Haussmann cuttings, which genuinely have more to do with town-planning than with class struggle, fitting into the urban fabric without devastating the quarters affected. Thus, on either side of the Rue Turbigo, the old revolutionary *section* of the Gravilliers on one side and the pretty Rues Meslay, du Vert-Bois and Notre-Dame-de-Nazareth on the other remain almost unchanged – as likewise, either side of the Rue de Rennes, do the ancient Rues du Vieux-Colombier, du Four, du Sabot and the little Rue Bernard-Palissy which has long been the home of Éditions de Minuit. People have forgotten that these streets were formerly working class. It was only in the course of the twentieth century that they passed into the hands of the well-to-do bourgeoisie, when living in old buildings became a modern fashion. Until the First World War and perhaps even into the 1930s, those with sufficient means lived in the good districts. Proust lived on Boulevard Malesherbes, Rue de Courcelles, Boulevard Haussmann, Rue Hamelin, and his characters dwell in the *hôtels* of the Faubourg Saint-Germain, or more often in the newer and elegant quarters of the 8th and 17th arrondissements. Only an eccentric like Swann would prefer the Quai d'Orléans on the Île Saint-Louis.

From Châtelet, a few steps are sufficient to reach what remains of the great church of Saint-Jacques-de-la-Boucherie, the Tour Saint-Jacques. By day, this is a Gothic vestige that was perhaps more beautiful when wrapped in scaffolding ('the prodigious scaffolding of monuments under repair, applying to the solid body of the architecture their modern architecture of such paradoxical beauty', as Baudelaire wrote[2]). But by night it is a different story. The tower is transfigured, standing out against the black background like a fantastic apparition. André Breton mentions it several times, for example in his poem 'Vigilance':

> The tottering Saint Jacques tower in Paris
> In the semblance of a sunflower
> Strikes the Seine sometimes with its forehead and its shadow glides
> Imperceptibly among the riverboats...

A poem he revisits in *Mad Love*: 'You may well have known that I loved this tower, I still see at this moment a whole violent existence organized around it to understand us, to contain the distraught in its cloudy gallop around us.' And the final chapter of *Arcanum 17* is completely devoted to it:

> It is certainly true that my mind has often prowled around that tower, for me very powerfully charged with occult significance, either because it shares in the doubly veiled life (once because it disappeared, leaving behind it this giant trophy, and again because it embodied as nothing else has, the sagacity of the hermeticists) of the Church of Saint-Jacques-de-la-Boucherie, or because it is endowed with legends about Flamel returning to Paris after his death.[3]

At the time when the immense church of Saint-Jacques was erected at the heart of the butchery quarter, the roadway on its eastern side was not yet called Rue Saint-Martin, but Rue Planche-Mibray towards the Seine, then Rue des Arcis as far as the Rue de la Verrerie. In June 1848, the barricade on the Rue Planche-Mibray was under the command of a sixty-year-old shoemaker named Voisambert.[4]

After the Rue de Rivoli, the Rue Saint-Martin leads to another battlefield, where the epilogue to the insurrection of 5–6 June 1832 took place. This uprising, which began with an immense crowd gathered behind the coffin of the republican general Lamarque, had been suppressed in the night of 5 June and the morning of the 6th. The last group of insurgents had retrenched to the Saint-Merri cloister, which became a real fortress. To understand what took place there, one should read the letter that Charles Jeanne, the head of the insurgents, wrote to his sister.[5] The centre of their stronghold was a house at no. 30 on the Rue Saint-Martin, with a system of three barricades around it, 'the first at the corner of the Rue Saint-Merri continued outward and cut the Rue Saint-Martin at a right angle; the second, also at a right angle to the former, blocked the Rue Aubry-le-Boucher; and finally the third, raised at the corner of the Rue Maubuée, brought this latter street within our retrenchments'. On several occasions, the National Guard were repelled, leaving dozens of dead on the roadway ('Then they were no longer a disciplined body, but a cloud of Cossacks in complete rout'), and it was only the artillery, firing simultaneously through the Rue Aubry-le-Boucher and along the Rue Saint-Martin from Saint-Nicolas-des-Champs, that reduced this stronghold. Jeanne and a dozen of his followers managed to beat a path by means of bayonets across the troop of assailants. It was on this 6 June that cannon were used for the first time against the people of Paris – the Lyon silk weavers had already had experience of this the previous year.

This insurrection aroused both interest and fascination on the part of several contemporary writers, whereas the events of June 1848, though far more threatening to the established system, as well as far more deadly, had no

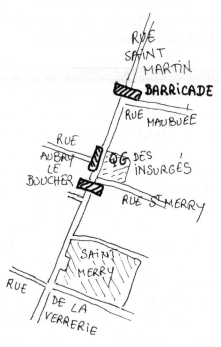

literary echo at the time – the silence of repression.[6] The underlying reason for this difference seems clear. While the men of June 1848 were, as we saw, anonymous proletarians who interested no one, the combatants of June 1832 included a number of students, sons of the bourgeoisie, as Stendhal ironically refers to in the opening lines of *Lucien Leuwen*: 'He had been expelled from the Polytechnique for having gone for an inappropriate walk, on a day that he and all his fellow students were detained; that was the time of one of the famous days of June, April or February 1832 or 1834.' Lucien was the favoured son of a big Parisian banker, who 'gave dinners of the highest distinction, almost perfect, and yet was neither moral, boring, nor ambitious, but simply fanciful; he had a large number of friends'. (A question that arises here is why Stendhal chose 'Leuwen', an Alsatian variant of 'Lévy', for a family whom nothing in the book signals to be Jewish. Were 'Jew' and 'banker' so connected in people's minds at this time?)

Among those who wrote about the insurrection of 1832, Victor Hugo in *Les Misérables* comes first to mind, with the barricade on the Rue de la Chanverie where Gavroche dies, but this book was written thirty years after the events. At the time, the young Hugo was still the reactionary he would remain until June 1848, the date (and cause) of a political turn that would go so far as to lead him to support the defeated and persecuted Communards of 1871. In *Things Seen*, under the date 6–7 June 1832, we read:

> Riot around Lamarque's cortege. Madness drowned in blood. One day we shall have a republic, and when this comes of itself it will be fine. But let us not pluck in May the fruit that will not be ready until July; let us know how to wait. The republic proclaimed by France in Europe will be the crown of our white hairs. But we should not let boors stain our flag red.

The *juste milieu*, to say the least, and a contrast with what Heine wrote in one of his reports for the *Augsburger Allgemeine* newspaper: 'It was the best blood of France which ran in the Rue Saint-Martin, and I do not believe that there was better fighting at Thermopylae than at the mouth of the Alley of Saint-Méry and Aubrey-des-Bouchers [*sic*].'[7]

The pre-eminent writer of this time, Chateaubriand, wrote in Book 35 of his *Mémoires*:

> General Lamarque's cortege led to two blood-stained days and the victory of Quasi-Legitimacy over the Republican Party. The latter, fragmented and disunited, carried out a heroic resistance. Paris was placed in a state of siege: it was censure on the largest possible scale, censure in the

style of the Convention, with this difference that a military commission replaced the revolutionary tribunal. In June 1832 they shot the men who brought them victory in July 1830; they sacrificed that same École Polytechnique, that same artillery of the National Guard, who had conquered the powers that be, on behalf of those who now struck at them, disavowed them and cast them off!

Admirable! Contempt for Louis-Philippe led Chateaubriand to accept the memory of the Convention – some actually said that the June insurgents included supporters of Charles X and the Duchesse de Berry.

In *Lost Illusions*, Michel Chrestien, the only honest and courageous republican in the whole of Balzac's *Comédie humaine*, is killed on the barricade of the Rue Saint-Merri: 'this gay bohemian of intellectual life, the great statesman who might have changed the face of the world, fell as a private soldier in the cloister of Saint-Merri'. He was buried in Père-Lachaise by his friends of the Cénacle who had taken the risk of coming to find his body on the battlefield.

There is no book by George Sand contemporary with these events (though she alludes to them in novels of the 1840s and in *The Story of My Life*). But in a letter to her friend Laure Decerfz, on 13 June 1832, she wrote:

To discover by the Seine below the Morgue [she lived on the Quai Saint-Michel] a red furrow, to see the straw that scarcely covers a heavy cart being spread, and to perceive under this crude wrapping twenty, thirty corpses, some in black and others in velvet jackets, all torn, mutilated, blackened by powder, sullied by mud and dried blood. To hear the cries of women who recognize their husbands and children here, all that is horrible.

There are other texts on the insurrection of 5–6 June 1832 besides those of the famous writers of the time. In September of the same year there appeared a novel entitled *Le Cloître Saint-Méry*, a love story set during the insurrection, and the work of a young author, Marius Rey-Dussueil, who worked for the republican paper *La Tribune*. The author was charged with provoking civil war and contempt for the royal government. He was acquitted in February 1833 but the book was destroyed by court order.

Agéno Altaroche, who was only twenty and not yet the poet and singer he would become, wrote a poem entitled '6 June! Mourning', which begins:

> Dead! Dead! They are no longer here, our brothers!
> Decease has closed their bloody eyelids
> They died side by side, all struck in the heart!
> See, see the great funerals pass . . .
> Here the echo on the fields of battle
> The ferocious cry of the conqueror!

Another young man, Hégésippe Moreau, who died of consumption a few years later, wrote a long poem entitled '5 and 6 June 1832', with the repeated refrain:

> They are all dead, the death of heroes,
> And despair is without weapons;
> At least against the executioners
> Let us have the courage of tears.

Let us imagine for a moment that the 'coming insurrection' goes badly: who will be found to honour those who are shot? A bad question that we should dismiss.

The part of the Rue Saint-Merri that served as a battle-field in 1832 now exists only in memory. It is possible all the same to observe here a rather infrequent phenomenon, two buildings abutting and even interpenetrating, one of which is an honest construction from the 1920s and another that might be called contemporary despite already being fifty years old. These are the municipal baths of the 4th arrondissement and Renzo Piano's IRCAM (Institut de Recherche et Coordination Acoustique/Musique), his first commission after the Beaubourg. I do not know whether the preservation of the baths was an architectural necessity or a deliberate choice. At all events, the way in which the IRCAM encompasses and respects these, the care taken to align the cornices of the one with the ironwork of the other, the intelligent decision to place the more modern façade towards the Stravinsky fountain designed by Tinguely and Niki de Saint Phalle rather than facing the Beaubourg, the choice of material – all this attests to an understanding modesty. As for the material, the small terracotta blocks that Piano used for the IRCAM (I am not sure whether we can call them 'bricks') are almost the same colour and exactly the same thickness as the bricks of the baths:

> We took particular care to place the tower in its context. The reminder of the Beaubourg is apparent at the top, the bare steel structure at the top of the lift cage and the network of aluminium supports for the glasswork and cladding. The opaque portion facing the corner of the square is of the same brick-red colour as the adjacent building [the bathhouse]. In any case, there is no question here of a visible wall, but of panels in terracotta. The terracotta element affixed to concealed bars is spaced by aluminium elements that form the only visible part of the fixture. The elements of the façade naturally resemble the neighbouring bricks in terms of their texture and colour. To accentuate the effect, we had them worked,

horizontally incised, to give the same perception in terms of their dimensions. A small example of artisanal attention to decoration, which contributes to strengthening the link of the building to its environment.[8]

Piano went on to use this material on many subsequent occasions, particularly in Paris for the housing ensemble on the Rue de Meaux.

Was it legitimate to name this centre, the Piano and Rogers building, after Pompidou, rather than the expressway on the Right Bank? I would say both yes and no. Yes, as Pompidou championed the creation of a great centre of contemporary art on the site made available by the destruction of Les Halles. He organized a genuine competition – very different from the masquerade mounted by Delanoë in 2002 for the renovation of the site – and accepted the jury's decision. And no, as the Piano and Rogers project was in no way to his liking. His artistic tastes were those of a provincial bourgeois who read *Le Figaro Magazine* (his office was decorated by Agam), and the 'hippy' character of the two winning contestants, who arrived at the ceremony tieless, in shorts (Piano) and yellow shirt (Rogers), was equally uncongenial.[9] It was Jean Prouvé, the president of the jury, who was responsible for the triumph of these two quite unknown architects more than thirty years ago. There was at least a tacit connivance between them: Piano and Rogers knew and admired Prouvé's work, and as the pioneer of metal architecture he could not fail to be seduced by their audacious 'Meccano' construction, and the great difference this represented from the Beaux-Arts style that was flourishing at the time (and indeed still flourishes today).

The opposition to going ahead with the prize-winning project did not come from Pompidou, but from the prefect. Piano and Rogers had had the idea, as important for them as the architecture itself, of not using the entire space available: 'We wanted to create a plaza, a kind of clearing, whose life would be complementary to the activities proposed at the Centre . . . Without bystanders, fire-eaters and street traders the plaza would not be what it is. It is thanks to the plaza that the Centre genuinely belongs to the city.' Built in a conch shape like the plaza outside the Palazzo Publico in Siena, the slope of the plaza leads gently towards the doors of the Centre. This required the segment corresponding to the Rue Saint-Martin to be pedestrianized, but:

> In the early 1970s the car was master of Paris. There were no pedestrian streets, and the public authorities allowed traffic and parking almost everywhere. The Paris prefecture was particularly hostile to a project that would extend a pedestrianized Rue Saint-Martin towards the Centre. The Rue Saint-Martin, continued by the Rue Saint-Jacques, formed the north-south axis of the capital, which there could be no question of interrupting by banning traffic. 'The Rue Saint-Martin is the longest street in Paris', the prefect kept saying. 'You cannot cut off the longest street in Paris, it's impossible!'

The great building, inaugurated in 1977, was for a long while a place for the people. There was no control on entry, in the hall you met all kinds of characters, sometimes with a can of beer in their hand, and guys from the banlieue could take the escalator to admire the view over Paris from the fifth floor. This was in line with what the creators intended: 'In the end, it's not that important for the Centre Pompidou to contain a museum or a library. The main thing is for people to meet here, in a certain everyday way, without having to pass through a gate and being checked like in a factory. It was to promote contact, to mix genres, to mingle different activities, that we imagined a giant Meccano construction overlooking the city.' When the Centre was renovated in 2010–12, all this was brought to order: the Vigipirate security system helped sort out entrants, the hall was redesigned to discourage loafers, the escalator is now accessible only with a ticket for the exhibitions, and the dishes on offer in the fifth-floor restaurant cost around 30 euros. We're now with the right class of people.

Perhaps this is not the worst retreat from the Centre's original design and its functioning in its early years. Like many other people, I can remember the exhibitions in the late 1970s mounted by a Swedish neo-Dadaist named Pontus Hulten. You came out of the *Paris–New York, Paris–Berlin* and *Paris–Moscow* exhibitions quite intoxicated, your only regret not still being inside. Since that time the level of exhibitions at the Centre has followed a steadily declining curve, ending up at the time I am writing with a celebration of the work of Jeff Koons, the most costly artist in the world thanks to his inflatable rabbits and little sugar pigs, or a Le Corbusier exhibition whose theme is 'the measure of man', carefully avoiding any debate on either the master's political friendships or his more debatable projects, such as the Voisin plan that envisaged the destruction of Paris.[10] Have we touched bottom? Let's wait and see.

CHAPTER 5

In Balzac's day, the tiny Rue de Venise, perpendicular to the Rue Saint-Martin opposite Beaubourg, was much longer than it is now, ending in a cul-de-sac close to the Rue Saint-Denis, to which it was linked by the Cour Batave. This series of three courts, famous at the time, is described by Balzac in *César Birotteau*, part of which takes place in and around Les Halles:

> This monastic construction, with arcades and internal galleries, built of cut stone and ornamented with a fountain at the back, a damaged fountain that opens its lion's maw less to give water than to request it from all passers-by, was in all likelihood invented to endow the Saint-Denis quarter with a kind of Palais-Royal. This unhealthy monument, buried on each of its four sides by high buildings, has only life and movement during the day; it is the centre of dark passages that meet each other and join the quarters of Les Halles and Saint-Martin via the famous Rue Quincampoix – damp paths where people in a hurry get rheumatism. There are several industrial cesspits, very few Batavians and many groceries.

Walking straight ahead, at a good pace, it should not take more than a quarter of an hour to get from Beaubourg to the Grands Boulevards, but it is better to go slowly so as to perceive the succession of strata between what remains of the old Halles and the Strasbourg-Saint-Denis intersection – a concentrate of Parisian history.

The Rue Quincampoix is a good starting point. The buildings on it have not changed much since the time of the regency of Louis XV, when the Scotsman John Law established his bank there and applied the famous 'principle' that enabled him to rise from an adventurer to superintendent of royal finances: the issue of paper money against gold. The regent, Philippe d'Orléans, faced with the threatening bankruptcy of the royal treasury (its debt being equivalent to ten years' tax receipts), authorized Law to issue quantities of paper money far greater than its gold coverage. So much so that in 1720 the system collapsed, when it became apparent that the famous paper was no longer worth anything. According to legend, in the days of its splendour a hunchback in the Rue Quincampoix hired himself out as a platform for those pressing to subscribe to shares in Law's bank.

The Hôtel de Beaufort, where Law had his office, disappeared with the cutting of Rue Rambuteau that leads to Rue Saint-Denis. Rambuteau, prefect of the Seine department under Louis-Philippe, opened up this street that rightly bears his name and undertook major work in the city, including the general extension of gas lighting and the levelling of the Grands Boulevards. It is to him that we owe such fine canyons overlooked by raised pavements as the Boulevard du Temple and the Boulevard Saint-Martin.

On the Rue Saint-Denis, where the Rue Rambuteau comes out, we again find Auguste Blanqui. We left him a very old man in his last dwelling on the boulevard that bears his name. Here he is a twenty-four-year-old student receiving his baptism of fire. On the night of 19 November 1827, following the electoral victory of the opposition in Paris, young people, so-called *casseurs*, threw stones at windows, including the police station on the Rue Mauconseil, and set up barricades made of planks and cobbles by the Saint-Leu church, the Passage du Grand-Cerf and the Rue Grénéta. These same rowdies repeated their misdeeds the following night, and the prefect of police had to send troops to restore order. They fired, killing four people, and the young Blanqui was among those injured, receiving a flesh wound in the shoulder, though this was not serious and was treated by his mother. The prefect concluded: 'These events have aroused in the quarter a salutary fear, which it is to be hoped will prevent the return of similar disorder.' A hope, we have to say, that was not fulfilled.[1]

In actual fact, the tradition of such riots was already well anchored in the Rue Saint-Denis. In 1709, a year of scarcity at the end of Louis XIV's reign, Saint-Simon relates:

> It happened that this Tuesday morning, 20 August, bread was lacking in many places. In the Saint-Denis quarter, a woman shouted out, exciting others. The archers positioned at the distribution points threatened this woman, who only shouted louder. They seized her and put her in shackles. Within a moment, all the artisans on the boulevard ran up, tore off her shackles and ran through the streets pillaging bakers and pastry shops; one after another, the shops closed. The disorder grew and spread to adjacent streets, without acts of violence; people demanded bread and everywhere they took it.[2]

The nights of November 1827 look like a dress rehearsal for the revolution of July 1830. On the 28th of this month, the second day of the 'Trois Glorieuses', a military column set off from the Innocents market, charged with clearing the quarter through the Rue Saint-Denis as far as the city gate. The task was not simple:

The battalion, armed with two artillery pieces that the difficulties of passage and the narrowness of the street made useless, immediately encountered most serious difficulties as soon as it left the Place des Innocents. It was rapidly separated from the rest of the column by barricades raised behind it, obstructed by those that it found ahead, and harassed by constant fire coming from windows on the Rue Saint-Denis. Level with the Rue Batave, in particular, there was a formidable barricade. The battalion crossed it only to come under fire from the rioters massed behind the gates of the Cour Batave, in which each window was a firing point.[3]

The street was blocked by a good thirty barricades (in those memorable days there were more than 4,000 throughout Paris).

In the many riots and insurrections under the July monarchy, the Rue Saint-Denis erupted every time. In June 1831, when the archbishop's palace was sacked:

On the 17th, 1,200 soldiers were posted, but they could not be trusted. They stayed drinking with the mutineers in the bars of the Rues Saint-Martin and Saint-Denis, and were in a continual state of intoxication. Around nine o'clock in the evening, cavalry charges in the Rue Neuve-Saint-Denis and the surrounding streets. There were many arrests.[4]

In the same year, on 7 September:

Warsaw had just been taken by the Russians and reduced to capitulation. When the sad news reached the capital, the people rose up and the revolutionary disturbances that are always latent resumed with particular intensity.

The crowd gathered outside the ministry of foreign affairs to cries of 'Long live Poland!' 'Down with the ministers!' Dispersed by the dragoons, the rioters took themselves off to the Porte Saint-Denis, the headquarters of the riot.

The Saint-Denis quarter rose up again at the time of the cholera epidemic of 1832, then during the insurrection that, as we saw, followed the burial of General Lamarque in June the same year, and once again in the course of the riot that followed the passing of the law of February 1834 that restricted freedom of the press (the massacre on the Rue Transnonain took place during this disturbance). The insurrection of May 1839 organized by the Société des Saisons (Blanqui, Barbès, Voyer d'Argenson, Laponneraye) had its nerve centre on the Rue Grénéta.

Alongside these 'historical' events in which the Rue Saint-Denis always played a major role, the quarter also rose up in small-scale riots that were brief, anonymous and soon forgotten:

On 12 September 1841, around eight in the evening, a gathering of some 300 individuals aged from sixteen to twenty, dressed in work clothes, stationed themselves on the Place du Châtelet crying out: 'Down with Louis-Philippe!' 'Long live the Republic!', 'Down with Guizot!' The forces of order managed to disperse them after serious clashes, in the course of which an officer of the peace was seriously injured. From the Place du Châtelet, the crowd took Rues Saint-Denis, Mauconseil, du Ponceau and Saint-Martin towards the Boulevard Saint-Martin, shouting out abuse. Some clothing shops were pillaged in passing. Red material was seized to make flags, with sticks taken from concierge lodges.[5]

The red flag had made its appearance on the insurrectionary side in the days of June 1832, a nice reversal of meaning, as it had previously been the signal announcing the proclamation of martial law.

Between the Rue Rambuteau and the monumental gate where it ends, the Rue Saint-Denis has neither the same architectural style throughout nor the same ambience. In an initial segment, as far as the intersection with the Rue Étienne-Marcel and the Rue Turbigo, it is still noisy and busy, takeaways jostling with second-hand clothing and sex toys. Nineteenth-century buildings break the continuity of older ones. The church of Saint-Leu-Saint-Gilles, which dates from the fourteenth century, has suffered many assaults that have left it a building quite lacking in grace. During the Revolution, on 29 Brumaire of year II, the Lombards section sent an address to the Convention announcing that 'it no longer recognizes any divinity other than Reason, and is bringing the treasures of superstition, amassed by hypocrisy, which will better serve to consolidate the Republic than to ornament lies'.[6] Following this, the church became a depot of salted meat for the sausage-makers of the quarter. When its function was restored, its apse unfortunately faced directly onto the Boulevard Sébastopol. Commissioned with remedying this, Victor Baltard demolished three chapels and closed the church on this side with a flat neo-Renaissance wall that at least has the merit of being unremarkable.

Between the Rue Turbigo and the Rue Réamur everything changes. The buildings here follow with calm regularity, I would even say a gentleness that makes this section a haven, a rest for the eyes. The majority of them were built under the Empire, the Restoration or the July monarchy, in other words, in the first half of the nineteenth century. The decrees on house alignment issued then, and the new sites available – church property that had been nationalized and divided

up during the Revolution – explain why the street was renovated at this time. All these buildings have common features
that give a sense of regular harmony: their height (four storeys), their narrow unshuttered windows, their flat façades
without balconies and almost without ornament, the alignment of their cornices, and finally their roughcast stucco – a
creamy off-white that is the true colour of the city, alongside
the grey of raw stone I have mentioned above. It is a miracle,
in any case, that the generations of builders who succeeded
each other on the scaffolding, at one time from the Creuse
and now from Mali, have been able to preserve this colour.
I continue here past traditional Paris shops, a few fine old
cafés, a newsagent, a wine-merchant, several haberdashers
– we are at the edge of the Sentier. The population is neither
bourgeois nor uniformly white: warehousemen, '*garçons de
boutique*' as they are called in the police report written after
the insurrection of 1827, building workers, and already the
female sex workers who are increasingly numerous as you
approach the Porte Saint-Denis.

A number of arcades connect the Rue Saint-Denis with
its adjoining streets: the narrow and tortuous Passage de la
Trinité leading to the Rue de Palestro, built on the site of the
Enfants-Bleus hospital (blue on account of their uniform,
not from one of those infantile heart diseases whose surgical treatment was for a long time my everyday task), the
little Passage Basfour, and especially the local wonder that
attracts a few tourists, the Passage du Grand-Cerf. Covered
over around 1825, it was until then the exit from the hos-
telry of the Grand Cerf onto the Rue Saint-Denis. It was
from this inn that diligences, coaches and carriages left for
towns north of Paris. In the opening pages of *A Start in Life*,
Balzac describes an establishment of this kind (located, it is
true, a little further up, on the corner of Rue du Faubourg-
Saint-Denis and Rue d'Enghien):

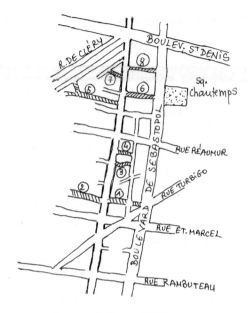

1 Passage de Bourg l'Abbé
2 Passage du Grand Cerf
3 Passage de la Trinité
4 Passage Basfour
5 Passage du Caire
6 Passage du Ponceau
7 Passage Sainte-Foy
8 Passage Lemoine

The Hôtel du Lion d'Argent occupies a piece of land which is very deep for its width. Though its frontage has only three or four windows on the Faubourg-Saint-Denis, the building extends back through a long courtyard, at the end of which are the stables, forming a large house standing close against the division wall of the adjoining property. The entrance is through a sort of passageway beneath the floor of the second storey, in which two or three coaches had room to stand.

But already in the very first lines, Balzac warned us:

> Railroads, in a future not far distant [this was written in
> 1842], must force certain industries to disappear forever,
> and modify several others, more especially those relating
> to the different modes of transportation in use around
> Paris. Therefore the persons and things which are the ele-
> ments of this scene will soon give to it the character of an
> archaeological work.

He was right, and it is in fact hard to imagine the Rue Saint-
Denis as it was in the 1840s: the major axis of north-south
traffic in Paris, along with the Rue Saint-Martin. A large
number of horse-drawn buses passed along it, belonging
to various companies: the Tricycles, running between the
Place des Victoires and the Bastille; the Diligentes, one from
the Rue Saint-Lazare to Charenton; the Citadines from
the Place des Petits-Pères to Belleville; the Écossaises from
Notre-Dame-des-Victories to the Halle aux Vins.

The Grand-Cerf has glass panels said to be the tallest
in all the Paris arcades, allowing for two levels above the
shops, the first for storage and the second for housing. (It is
sometimes said that Céline spent his childhood there, and
that the Grand-Cerf was the model for the Bérézinas arcade
in *Death on Credit*, but this was in fact the Passage Choiseul.) As in many of the Paris arcades, the shops – furniture,
candles, jewellery, African art – are by no means fashionable. Let's hope that they remain this way, slightly dusty
and a little sad.

Taking the Passage du Grand-Cerf and then the Rue
Marie-Stuart, I reach the Rue Montorgueil, opposite the
Stohrer patisserie that has offered the most exquisite mac-
aroons ever since the reign of Louis XV. This is one of the
charms of the big city: in less than two hundred metres you

cross from the Rue Saint-Denis, a working-class fragment of old Paris, to the Rue Montorgueil, one of those most frequented by a young and well-heeled bourgeoisie, and by tourists from around the world.

Reaching the Rue Réamur, I am struck by a very clear frontier effect. This is not due to crossing from the 1st to the 2nd arrondissement. These arrondissements have only a weak identity; 'I live in the 5th arrondissement' has a clear meaning, but no one says 'I live in the 2nd', as opposed to 'close to the Bourse' or 'behind the Bibliothèque Nationale'. If the Rue Réamur forms a frontier, this is because its two sides are so different here that by crossing from one to the other you actually change worlds. The south side is a mixture of old buildings, post-Haussmann constructions and eclecticism. The huge Félix Potin building, between the Boulevard Sébastopol and the Rue de Palestro, brings a touch of Art Nouveau, with its octagonal rotunda topped by a skylight that it would be nice to be able to climb up to. Monoprix should be taken to task for replacing the venerable signboard that was still prominent in the 1980s. We also owe Félix Potin another great Art Nouveau building, one of the rare beauties on the Rue de Rennes.

The road parallel with the Rue Réamur to the south is called after Pierre Lazareff. The newspaper *France-Soir*, whose last owner was a Russian oligarch, has finally bit the dust, so I can say without injury to anyone what this paper represented. Under the editorship of Pierre Lazareff, as part of the Hachette group, *France-Soir* proclaimed itself 'the only French newspaper with over a circulation over a million', and played the same role that the TF1 television channel does today: working to brainwash the greatest number of people, while earning as much money as possible. It was supine towards governments of any shade, with only one column saving its honour, the crosswords of Max

Favalelli. If Lazareff is today seen as a great journalist, this is a collateral effect of the cult of the 1960s, the heyday of the 'Trente Glorieuses', a golden age that we are told will return one day – whereas the Gaullist years were actually ones of conformity and boredom on the one hand, and of war and police brutality on the other, ignominies that Pierre Lazareff and *France-Soir* covered with regular servility.

The north side of the Rue Réamur is as rectilinear, homogeneous and solid as the south side is mixed and imaginative. It consists of a regular series of long buildings in a style that could be called 'commercial monumental', the oldest dating from 1900 and the most recent from the 1930s, when the rag trade was still a flourishing industry: in the street, in shops, and in the two or three upper levels of workshops and stores. Some of these buildings were successful, like the two with rotunda and dome that majestically frame the entry to the Rue Dussoubs. (Named after Denis Dussoubs, deputy in the legislative assembly of the Second Republic, killed on the Mauconseil barricade on 4 December 1851 while resisting the coup d'état of Louis Bonaparte. Victor Hugo relates his heroic death in *History of a Crime*.)

North of the Rue Réamur, the Rue Saint-Denis changes in both construction style and atmosphere. There are still many buildings similar to those described above, but the alignment is no longer respected, and is mixed in with post-Haussmann buildings, taller and often set back. This is the ready-to-wear end of the rag trade, and sex workers are more numerous. (I have used this term since we published the book by Thierry Schaffauer, who practises this profession and is often in this quarter.[7])

The historical vestiges of this segment of the Rue Saint-Denis are only virtual: the crossing in the wall of Charles V just before reaching the Boulevard Saint-Denis (whereas the wall of Philippe Auguste was crossed level with the Rue

Étienne-Marcel); the memory of the great convent of the Filles de l'Union Chrétienne on the corner with the Rue de Tracy, where the statue of a smiling Michelet, in bas-relief and standing, recalls that his father had established his printing works in the church of the confraternity, and that Jules was born there in 1798.

The arcades here are many and varied. The Passage Saint-Foy, very narrow and dark, is often occupied by ladies who do not want to be disturbed in their activities. The wretched Passage du Ponceau comes out on the Boulevard Sébastopol opposite the Square Émile-Chautemps – a Radical senator under the Third Republic, this public garden devoted to him being one of the finest from nineteenth-century Paris. The two basins decorated with sculptures, either mythological or 'of their time' (Agriculture, Industry), the perfectly designed cast-iron balustrades around the lawns, the quite simple wooden benches, the gardeners' huts, the great chestnut trees, and the spacious setting between the Conservatoire des Arts et Métiers and the façade of the Gaîté-Lyrique theatre, make this an ideal halt in a quarter that does not have many such. Above I made a list of my favourite Paris public gardens of the 1930s. There are just as many successful ones from the 1850s, mainly the work of the Davioud-Alphand team, such as the Square Louvois opposite the Bibliothèque Nationale, the Square Montholon off the Rue La Fayette, or the Square Paul-Painlevé between the Sorbonne and the Cluny museum. With their old trees, their fountains, their statues and their lawns (no walking!), they are old-fashioned and peaceable places, well suited to the student's sandwich or the pensioner's cigarette.

In this segment of the Rue Saint-Denis, the courtyards remind me of those of the Marais of my childhood, dark, dirty and encumbered with carts, lean-tos with tin roofs, vans – the same courtyards that you have today outside the most

Eugéne Atget, Place du Caire, *1903.*

expensive apartments and most elegant shops in the city. Here the decrepitude is less marked – the obligatory face-lift has passed them by – but there is the same contrast between the nobility of the stone and the quite plebeian activities.

Between the Rue du Caire and the Rue d'Alexandrie, the Rue Saint-Denis borders the Passage du Caire, doyen of Parisian arcades, opened in 1799 after Bonaparte's return from the expedition to Egypt. The Egyptomania of the time can be traced in the street names – Alexandrie, Damiette, Aboukir, Le Caire – as well as in the proud façade of the main entry on the Place du Caire, decorated with three heads of the goddess Hathor. The Passage du Caire is not only the oldest arcade, it is also totally different from all the other Paris arcades. Whether they are more fashionable, like Véro-Dodat, Colbert, Vivienne, or more down-market like Choiseul or Jouffroy, these are places to stroll, to buy fancy goods or books, to stop for coffee – in other words, as Walter Benjamin put it, 'The arcade is a street of lascivious commerce only; it is wholly adapted to arousing desires.'[8] The Passage du Caire, however, is nothing like that at all. It is not made for the casual walker, and no tourists are to be found. Its activity is the wholesale trade in fabrics, in ready-to-wear, and in supplies for shop windows – models, stands, decorations and packaging, which is not so far removed from its original activities, such as the printing of calico. The trade is solidly maintained by Sephardic Jews, and the only café-restaurant, Le Beverly, states that it is under Lubavitch supervision. The interest of this arcade lies not in its displays, but in its architecture, its glass panels, its complicated arrangement. Although its overall plan is rectangular, its galleries are disposed in a star, and it has no less than six entrances, on the Place du Caire, the Place d'Alexandrie, the Rue du Caire (three in all) and the Rue Saint-Denis. In the mornings in front of these entries you can see Pakistanis and Sri Lankans leaning on their trolleys, waiting to be hired for errands or by the hour to load lorries or shift stocks. It is the client who sets the price, and negotiation is clearly not simple for these new slaves, many of whom are probably without residence papers.

I remember having had one day in the Rue du Caire a kind of hallucination, seeing in the distance a Gothic rose window whose presence was inexplicable and almost disturbing. Glued to the spot, it took me a moment to understand. What I was seeing was the former priory of Saint-Martin-des-Champs – since 1794 the Conservatoire des Arts et Métiers – not far as the crow flies but at such a mental distance that it had been impossible to identify it at first glance. Every attentive Parisian has such strange things in their visual repertoire, the most well-known of these being the view of the Sacré-Coeur above Notre-Dame-de-Lorette as seen from the Rue Laffitte. These can be mere optical illusions, such as that which disturbs me each morning when I walk to the offices of La Fabrique along the Rue du Général-Lasalle. This street, a steep incline, comes out into the Rue Rébeval at an obtuse angle – this detail being decisive for what follows. On the side opposite the Rue Rébeval, facing you as you walk uphill, is a five-storey garage, covered in white roughcast to the front and clad with red brick on the side wall, which you see slightly on the bias. The strange thing is that the angle formed by the two walls of the garage appears not to be straight, failing to obey the rules of perspective set by Brunelleschi, Alberti and Piero della Francesca. The top storey, which emerges above the adjacent buildings, seems rather like one of those lop-sided kiosks in which Giotto's sacred scenes take place. Then, when the white wall is no longer illuminated by the morning sun, everything is restored to order.

In their final portion before the Grand Boulevards and the *portes*, the Rue Saint-Denis, the Boulevard Sébastopol and

The Sacré-Coeur above Notre-Dame-de-Lorette, as seen from the Rue Laffitte.

the Rue Saint-Martin advance in parallel, in a valley framed by two heights. Sloping streets climb up from this: on the Saint-Martin side the Rue Meslay, and on the Saint-Denis side the Rue de la Lune, the Rue Chénier and the stairs of the Rue des Degrés. Yet this is not the bed of any watercourse. There is nothing natural about the relief, it is entirely the result of human activity. From Charles V to Louis XIV, Paris was surrounded by a fortified wall that followed the line of the present boulevards from the Bastille to the Porte Saint-Denis, then turned towards the Louvre in a straight line along the Rues de Cléry and d'Aboukir (the sharp difference in level between these two streets is due to the rampart: Rue de Cléry, the higher one, corresponds to the top of this, and Rue d'Aboukir to its ditch). In the 1670s, Louis XIV decided to demolish the wall and replace it with a boulevard right around the city, planted with a double line of trees. This was a colossal project, since the wall was both high and thick, having been further reinforced in the late sixteenth century by the supporters of the Ligue, when they defended Paris against the royal troops. The amount of debris was enormous, and there could be no question of moving it away, given the means of the time. It is the accumulation of this that today forms the hills around the Strasbourg-Saint-Denis intersection. The western hill was for a long time known as the '*butte aux gravois*', and it is probably on account of the instability of its artificial subsoil that the bell-tower of Notre-Dame-de-Bonne-Nouvelle leans slightly.

Until not so long ago, the incline of the Rue Meslay was still the almost exclusive domain of artisanal footwear, which has declined somewhat in the face of factory products but remains present in this working-class street. At the top, the stairs of the pretty Passage du Pont-aux-Biches lead down to the Rue Notre-Dame-de-Nazareth, where fine groceries, children's clothing, design galleries and elegant hairdressers are so many signs of the rampant gentrification of the part of this quarter that adjoins the Marais. The third of these parallel streets, the Rue du Vert-Bois, only just escaped a disaster. A very rich man had the plan of making it the most fashionable and expensive street in Paris. He bought up several shops to establish galleries and luxury restaurants. The latest information is that his plan has failed, but many of the shop fronts of former pharmacies, bakers or haberdashers are still closed behind grilles, and the street has a desolate look.

On the other side of the valley, beyond the Rue Saint-Denis, the Rue Poissonnière, Rue de Cléry and Boulevard de Bonne-Nouvelle define a very particular hill. True, this is geographically part of the Sentier quarter, but the early seventeenth-century streets are so narrow that it is hard going for delivery vehicles, hence a certain calm in this crowded and busy district. The slender André Chénier building between the Rue Cléry and the Rue Beauregard – perhaps as often photographed as the Flatiron building on the corner of Broadway and Fifth Avenue; the very simple church where the funeral of poor Coralie took place at the end of *Lost Illusions*; the squashed shop fronts on the Rue Notre-Dame-de-Recouvrance; the view down to the Porte Saint-Denis from the Rue de la Lune: this little triangle is hardly a *quartier*, yet every stone here holds a memory, like that of Jeanne Poisson, born on the Rue de Cléry, who would become the Marquise de Pompadour.

Across the Rue Poissonnière I come into the heart of the Sentier, then, through the Rues de Jeûneurs and du Croissant, into what was still thirty years ago the press quarter. From *L'Humanité* to *Le Figaro*, all the papers had their editorial offices and printing works here – the sole exception being *Le Monde*, on the Rue des Italiens. As soon as the ink was dry, the deliverymen scattered in all directions on bicycles fixed with large front panniers, weighed down with impressive piles of newsprint. (Later, they drove BMW motorbikes, with the papers in a sidecar.) A plaque above the door of a large building on the Rue du Croissant, 'Imprimerie de la Presse', is the last vestige of this world, where lorries bringing rolls of paper for the presses caused memorable traffic jams.

In the days of June 1848, it was at the Porte Saint-Denis that the first shots were fired. This episode is described by two contemporaries who were not eye-witnesses – if I am not mistaken, none of the participants left a written record – yet their accounts concur. The first is Victor Hugo, who was one of the sixty representatives of the people charged with restoring the morale of the troops. *Things Seen*, Saturday 24 June:

> The National Guard, irritated more than intimidated, advanced in a rush to the barricade. At that moment, a woman appeared on top of the barricade, young, pretty, wild-haired and terrible. This woman, who was a prostitute, lifted her dress up to her belt and shouted to the National Guards, in the horrible brothel language that one always has to translate: 'Cowards, fire on the belly of a woman if you dare!' Events now took a terrifying course. The National Guard did not hesitate. A platoon-fire toppled the wretched woman; she fell with a loud scream. There was a horrible silence, both on the barricade and from the attackers. Suddenly a second woman appeared. This one was still younger and prettier: almost a child, scarcely seventeen years old. What a wretched situation! She too was a prostitute. She lifted her dress, showed her belly, and cried: 'Shoot, you brigands!' They shot. She fell in a hail of bullets on the body of the first. It was thus that the war began.

Hugo, as we see here, was not yet the defender of the people who would write *History of a Crime* three years later.

The second account is that of Daniel Stern, the pseudonym of Marie d'Agoult, a marquise and the companion of Franz Liszt. She was equally on the side of order, but it is clear that this is written by a woman:

I have said how Pujol [a major figure in the insurrection] had the first barricade constructed level with the Porte Saint-Denis. It was flanked by two others, which closed the entrance to the Rues de Mazagran and de Cléry. A detachment of around fifty men from the 2nd legion came down the boulevard, with drums beating the muster, not suspecting that the insurgents were so close until they found themselves unexpectedly facing the barricade. The National Guard showed that they were not firing, and continued to advance until about forty paces. But, either because their signal had not been understood, or because it had not been heeded, a fusillade from the terrace of a house on the corner of the Boulevard de Bonne-Nouvelle and the Faubourg-Saint-Denis hit them sideways; a dozen of them fell dead or wounded . . . Soon a battalion of the 2nd legion was seen to arrive, commanded by Lieutenant-Colonel Bouillon, along with a company from the 3rd legion. They were met with a terrible fire, but advanced steadily on the barricade; a second discharge forced them to retreat. A struggle began. There was fighting hand to hand; twelve National Guard were killed, and some forty others seriously wounded. Nothing however shattered their courage. The National Guard returned to the charge with vigour. The leader of the insurgents, who was directing the fire from on top of an upturned carriage, was struck by a bullet and fell. It seemed that the battle was over. But at the very moment that the flag fell from the leader, a young woman, who had not previously been visible, seized it. She raised it above her head and waved it with an inspired air. With thin hair and bare arms, in a strikingly coloured dress, she seemed to defy death. On seeing her, the National Guard hesitated to fire; they shouted to the young woman to get back; she remained undaunted, and provoked the attackers with her gestures and voice; a shot was fired, and she staggered and collapsed. But another woman suddenly rushed to her side; with one hand she supported the bloody body of her friend, with the other she hurled stones at the attackers. A new volley of shots echoed, and she fell in her turn on to the body that she was embracing.[9]

Who knows whether the ladies of the Rue Blondel will take part in the coming insurrection.

The project of a circular boulevard, designed by François Blondel and Pierre Bullet, involved the construction of the Porte Saint-Denis and the Porte Saint-Martin. Today these still focus and organize the Strasbourg-Saint-Denis intersection. They are linked by the short Boulevard Saint-Denis, between the Boulevard Saint-Martin on one side and the Boulevard Bonne-Nouvelle on the other. This is one of the two territories where Chinese sex workers practise, the other being the Boulevard de la Villette in the 19th arrondissement.

Blondel, the director of the project, was given the Porte Saint-Denis, the larger and more ornate of the pair, through which royal processions would pass. The bas-reliefs by François and Michel Anguier, on the theme of the victories of Louis XIV in Holland, are certainly a success, but the prevailing impression is of an enormous enterprise of sycophancy financed by Paris notables in the 1670s. My own preference is for Bullet's Porte Saint-Martin, smaller, less solemn, and in a gentler stone to which the vermicular embossment lends an almost Italian tone.

All the same, looking not so much at the gate itself as at what surrounds it, the advantage seems to me to lie with the Porte Saint-Denis. Not that the surroundings of the Porte Saint-Martin lack attractions: the theatres of the Renaissance and the Porte-Saint-Martin have fine façades, the Rue René-Boulanger serving as a corridor between them in an arc that follows a salient of the old rampart. And the perspective extends south towards the bell-tower of Saint-Nicolas-des-Champs, and north to the fine profile of the *mairie* of the 10th arrondissement and the windows of the Gare de l'Est.

The setting of the Porte Saint-Denis, however, has a kind of natural nobility, without either deliberate arrangement or planning. The two large buildings that frame the end of the Rue Saint-Denis, the magnificent balustrade of the Rue de la Lune, the perspective of the Boulevard Bonne-Nouvelle inseparable from the memory of André Breton ('Meanwhile, you can be sure of meeting me in Paris, of not spending more than three days without seeing me pass, toward the end of the afternoon, along the Boulevard Bonne-Nouvelle between the *Matin* printing office and the Boulevard de Strasbourg'),[10] the semicircle in the background where the faubourg begins, Le Petit Pot Saint-Denis where Gérard de Nerval was a regular customer – all these elements may seem disparate, yet they compose a landscape where I always feel one of the city's hearts beating, amid the din and exhaust fumes of the traffic.

Breton, Benjamin, Baudelaire, Nerval, Balzac, Chateaubriand – perhaps my references lack variety. But there is nothing I can do about it, this is my paper family, as good as any other. (It has other members as well, but too distant from my present itinerary: Diderot at the Palais-Royal,

Stendhal in Milan, Mallarmé on the Rue de Rome). Their books are the most worn ones on my shelves, their covers discoloured and their spines so tired that they stay open by themselves. I know so well where to find them that I can do so in the dark. The ties that link this artificial family are not only literary but also political. It may seem strange to make such a connection between Breton, whose sympathies ran more to Trotskyism, and such defenders of throne and altar as Balzac and Chateaubriand. Yet they did have, besides their proclaimed opinions, certain essential common characteristics: respect for the people and contempt for the 'elites'. Chateaubriand never forgot the humiliation he had felt in his youth, when, as an émigré from the petty Breton gentry in the army of the princes, he slept in a ditch and saw the brilliant carriages of the general staff roll pass. During the revolution of 1830, when the dynasty he tried to save collapsed, he was enchanted to be carried in triumph by students 'to cries of *Vive la Charte! Vive la liberté de la presse! Vive Chateaubriand!*'[11] And we have seen the respectful admiration with which he spoke of the insurgents of June 1832, whereas he had seen Charles X and his entourage as blind and blinkered. As for Balzac, we sense in him a real tenderness towards the poor, the disinherited, those left behind by life, whereas the harshness and corruption of the upper classes are a basic theme throughout *La Comédie humaine*. Here he is in *Ferragus* speaking of beggars, the lowest on the social scale:

> They often cause a laugh, but they always cause reflection. One represents to you civilization stunted, repressed; he comprehends everything, the honour of the galleys, patriotism, virtue, the malice of a vulgar crime, or the fine astuteness of elegant wickedness. Another is resigned, a perfect mimer, but stupid. All have slight yearnings after

order and work, but they are pushed back into their mire by society, which makes no inquiry as to what there may be of great men, poets, intrepid souls, and splendid organizations among these vagrants, these gypsies of Paris.

Balzac's preferred heroes are marginal characters, humiliated women or such saints as the good judge Popinot in *The Commission in Lunacy*, or Mme de La Chanterie in *The Brotherhood of Consolation*. Neither Chateaubriand nor Balzac speaks of the villainous mob, of alcohol-soaked and idle masses. True, both were men of order, and Christian compassion plays a part in their sentiment towards the people. But no matter, you never find with them that mixture of contempt and fear, the 'spites and acerbities ... the ancient bile of Flaubert, of the Goncourts, and of Gautier' that Sartre speaks of.[12] This may be seen as a difference bound up with the epoch, but it is not. These people, at table in the Magny restaurant, had a contemporary, Baudelaire – whom they rightly despised ('Baudelaire had supper at the next table to ours. He was wearing a cravat, his shirt open at the neck and his head shaved, just as if he were going to be guillotined. A single affectation: his little hands washed and cared for, the nails kept scrupulously clean. That face of a maniac, a voice that cuts like a knife, and a precise elocution that tries to copy Saint-Just and succeeds'[13]). And with Baudelaire, precisely as with Saint-Just ('The unfortunate are the powers of the earth'), it is love that one reads for the poor of both sexes, for 'The Little Old Women':

> Ruins! My family! My fellow-minds!
> Each evening I will bid a grave adieu!
> What of tomorrow, Eves of eighty years,
> Pressed by the dreadful talon of the Lord?

Or, in 'Morning Twilight':

> Poor old women, with chilled and meagre breasts,
> Blew the embers, then fingers, roused from rest.
> It was the hour, when frozen, with money scarcer,
> The pains of women in childbirth grew fiercer . . .

Or again for the father in 'The Eyes of the Poor', with his children in front of the café brightly lit by gas lamps; for 'The Widows', again poor ('The mourning of the poor always has something lacking, an absence of harmony that makes it more shattering. It is forced to skimp on its pain'). It was not accidental that Baudelaire should have placed Balzac above all the other writers of his age, and that the Goncourts saw him as a madman.

CHAPTER 6

Leaving the monumental gates for the region of the railway stations, you enter the faubourgs. As applied to Paris, this is an odd word, since if *fau* comes from the Latin *fors*, the characteristic of a faubourg is to be outside the city, whereas the Paris streets that bear this name are, if not central, at least well within the urban perimeter. This is of course a question of history. In the early eighteenth century, after crossing the tree-planted boulevard that marked the limit of Paris, you were in the country, where the major Paris streets continued along paths of beaten earth bordered by market gardens, vines and windmills. But Paris was very close, so much so that in the course of that century these earthen paths were paved and served as markers for an urbanization that advanced steadily from the centre despite royal decrees. It was these routes that would form the faubourgs, outside the official limits of the city until the end of Louis XVI's reign – hence their name – then included in Paris when the Wall of the Farmers-General shifted the boundary. Previously Paris had come to an end at the Bastille, the Porte Saint-Martin and the Tuileries, but it now extended via the Faubourg Saint-Antoine to the Barrière du Trône (now Place de la Nation), via the Faubourg Saint-Martin to the Barrière de La Villette (now Stalingrad), and via the Champs-Élysées to Étoile. The next leap, the annexation of the 'crown villages' in 1860 (Vaugirard, Passy, Les Batignolles, Montmartre, Belleville, etc.), ended up making the old faubourgs almost central. Yet in literature the ambiguity remained:

the faubourgs are very present in Baudelaire ('*Le faubourg secoué par les lourds tombereaux*' in 'The Seven Old Men', '*Au coeur d'un vieux faubourg, labyrinth fangeux*' in 'The Rag-Pickers' Wine', examples abound[1]), without our ever knowing their precise location. Much later, when Eugène Dabit wrote *Faubourgs de Paris* in 1933, he included the Rue de Ménilmontant, the Rue de Choisy-le-Roi and even the Rue de Montlhéry.

From the Porte Saint-Denis and the Porte Saint-Martin, the Rue du Faubourg-Saint-Denis, the Boulevard de Strasbourg and the Rue du Faubourg-Saint-Martin run almost parallel – 'almost', as the Rue du Faubourg-Saint-Denis bends a little towards the Gare du Nord, while the other two make a straight line towards the Gare de l'Est. Despite the short distance between them, each of these streets has its specific identity, population and beauty.

The Rue du Faubourg-Saint-Martin is open, airy, almost peaceful despite the traffic. As Thomas Clerc wrote in his book on the 10th arrondissement, 'all the buildings in this fine street, which escaped Haussmann, are different from one another – it is a faubourg, with its irregular curve and its rebel spirit'.[2] This book is almost ten years old and the street has changed: fewer ready-to-wear wholesalers, more boarded-up shops, more couscous and Chinese restaurants, and an increasing number of African hairdressers as you continue. On the right-hand pavement, Le Splendid, whose hour of glory goes back to the 1970s, now leads a discreet existence. Further along, the Passage du Marché opens onto a Haussmannian building that welcomes you with its sculpted décor, and leads to a pleasant *coin* (a *coin* being less than a *quartier* but more than a crossroads), a small open space bordered by the Saint-Martin market, an ugly building from the 1960s, a fire station and, on the corner with the Rue du Château-d'Eau, a good-quality brasserie, Le Réveil du 10e.

Between the barracks and the *mairie* of the 10th arrondissement, the little street called after Pierre Bullet is as chaste as that of his colleague Blondel, on the other side of the Porte Saint-Martin, is light, devoted as it is to tariffed love. The Rue Pierre-Bullet runs into the Rue Hittorff, tiny and ending in a kind of cul-de-sac. The Paris municipal counsellors did not do Hittorff proud, perhaps because he was 'Prussian'. The architect who renovated the Place de la Concorde, with the idea of centring it on the obelisk, who built the Cirque d'Hiver, the Théâtre du Rond-Pont des Champs-Élysées, the church of Saint-Vincent-de-Paul on the Rue La Fayette, the *mairie* of the 5th arrondissement as a pendant to Soufflot's Faculté de Droit, and such a masterpiece as the façade of the Gare du Nord, deserves better than this wretched little street.

The *mairie* of the 10th arrondissement, built in the 1890s, is a good culmination of nineteenth-century eclecticism. The objective is clear: a large building in French neo-Renaissance style, neo-Chambord if you like, more coherent and in my view more successful than the majority of Parisian *mairies*, which are indecisive and often lazy in style. Opposite it is the start of the Passage du Désir, with its almost monastic silence, low and regular buildings alternately in brick and white stone, which despite its name is a kind of Parisian convent. But its closed windows and its many boarded-up shop fronts lead us rather to fear the intentions of some developer or a semi-public company.

After its intersection with the Boulevard Magenta, the Rue du Faubourg-Saint-Martin widens, flaring to envelop the apse of the Saint-Laurent church on the left and the former convent of the Récollets, now the Maison de l'Architecture, on the right. From the large triangular square to the east side of the Gare de l'Est, it heads towards the rotunda of La Villette.

The Boulevard de Strasbourg is far from being merely a corridor for motor vehicles. We have to admit that it begins badly: of its four corners with the Boulevard Saint-Denis, two are occupied by banks, the third by a KFC (whose founder, as depicted on the logo, looks rather like Trotsky), and the fourth, presently a construction site, leads us to fear the worst. But very soon you encounter the pretty Théâtre Antoine, below whose triangular pediment are mosaics in lively colours that illustrate Comedy, Music and Drama. Opposite, on the corner with the Rue de Metz, is one of the finest Art Deco buildings in Paris, ornamented with golden peacock wings that sparkle in the sunshine.

The boulevard then bisects a roadway that that was built as a unity: on the right the Rue Gustave-Goublier and on the left the Passage de l'Industrie, entirely devoted to hair products, from wigs and hairpieces to perfumery. It ends with a Palladian window (three bays, with the centre one higher than the other two and topped by a semi-circular arch) before coming out on the Rue du Faubourg-Saint-Denis. A few metres further, also on both sides of the boulevard, is the famous Passage Brady. The left-hand section houses Pakistani and Indian restaurants beneath a glass roof with two continuous rows of panels. To the right is the famous costumier Sommier, who since 1922 has hired out every kind of uniform or disguise. You can emerge equally as a traditional policeman in a cape, a tango dancer or a Napoleonic general. When I was an intern in the 1960s, we would go there before parties. (Is there still this custom? To be sure, its disappearance would be no great loss, being as it was a mixture of machismo, crude humour and caste spirit.)

From the Passage Brady to the Rue du Château-d'Eau and beyond is the exclusive and unchallenged domain of African coiffure, a little bit of Africa in Paris, where touts practise their eloquence leaning against the Métro railings, where hairstylists work in shops of all colours, under names you might find in Cotonou or Lagos: 'Saint-Esprit Cosmétique' or 'God's Rock'. The whole African continent is represented, English-speakers as well as French – even Jamaicans. The ambience is noisy and friendly, even if there are times when you can no longer laugh: a fine short film by Sylvain George, *N'entre pas sans violence dans la nuit*, captures a moment of revolt when the whole quarter confronted the police and even repelled them for a while, showing that African inventiveness can find applications in many fields.

N'entre pas sans violence dans la nuit, *film by Sylvain George.*

Like the Rue du Faubourg-Saint-Martin, the Boulevard de Strasbourg widens into a large square in front of the Gare de l'Est, from which you can see several kilometres away the dome of the Tribunal de Commerce. This is the terminus for buses whose numbers start with '3': the 30 that runs to the Trocadéro, the 31 to the Étoile, the 32 to the Porte d'Auteuil, the 35 to the Mairie d'Aubervilliers, the 38 to the Porte d'Orléans. George Perec, in *Species of Spaces*, explains how to know where Paris bus lines start from their numbers (those beginning with '2' from the Gare Saint-Lazare, with '4' from the Gare du Nord, etc.). He even claims that the second digit also has a meaning, but here I think he exaggerates a little.

The Gare de l'Est, with its long colonnade, its glass canopy overlooked by statues of Verdun (on the right, with helmet) and Strasbourg (on the left), its low buildings, its pedestrianized paved court, is the most welcoming of the major Paris stations. It was almost provincially calm even, until the TGV de l'Est came into service. True, you can not complain that it no longer takes five hours to reach Strasbourg, but the station's east wing now houses a commercial centre in which 'brands' offer their usual displays. Let us remain in the hall of the 'Strasbourg departure', where a gigantic painting recalls less peaceful moments.

For those wishing to reach the Gare du Nord from here, the best route is the Rue d'Alsace. Above the twin flights of steps that make a fine oval, the street becomes a balcony over the railway. There has been here for a long time a bookshop very properly called La Balustrade, which was still orthodox communist until a few years ago. Since the death of its owner – whom I used regularly to see selling *L'Humanité Dimanche* when I lived on the Rue de Sofia – the window instead displays scientific books. On the corner of the Rue des Deux-Gares that leads towards the Rue du Faubourg-Saint-Denis, a café bears another well-found name: Au Train de Vie. Here you are already very close to the concrete lattices bordering the bridge on the Rue Gayette, from which Gilles Quéant jumped into thin air at the end of Jean Rouch's *Gare du Nord*.[3]

But let us return to the Porte Saint-Denis. On the corner between the Faubourg and the Boulevard Saint-Denis is a building from the 1880s. Beneath the second-storey balcony is the sculpture of a standing hooded figure, with the inscription 'Au grand Saint-Antoine'. He holds a book under his right arm, and his left hand is caressing a pig, which suggests that there used to be a charcuterie in the premises now occupied by an optician's. (There are several representations

Stairway, Rue d'Alsace.

of St Anthony accompanied by a tame pig – or boar?) What is certain is that the good old Paris charcuteries, with their mountains of celeriac remoulade, their breaded pig feet, their lobster halves and vol-au-vents, are in the process of disappearing, often replaced by their Chinese counterparts.

A few metres further is the entrance to the Passage du Prado, an L-shaped arcade whose other branch exits onto the Boulevard Saint-Denis. Some twenty years ago this was the domain of the sewing machine: new and second-hand, repairs, spare parts for all makes, threads, bobbins. No trace of this remains, perhaps because the more or less clandestine sewing workshops of eastern Paris that employed Chinese or Turkish workers have also gone. From two apartments in which I have lived, on the Rue du Faubourg-du-Temple and now on Rue Ramponeau, I have seen the disappearance of these nearby workshops, where the click of sewing machines echoed from morning to night. They have given way to the offices of architects, designers or photographers. The couture of the Sentier is very likely carried out today in what used to be called the Third World, and the Passage du Prado is rather decrepit, several of its shop fronts being closed, its activity reduced to a few African or Pakistani hairdressers.

After this passage, the Rue du Faubourg-Saint-Denis is the centre of a small Turkish quarter, or more accurately Turkish-Kurd. In the cafés and restaurants, the vegetable stores and even the pharmacy, you find the same welcome as in the Istanbul bazaar: a whiff of the Orient just a few steps from the Porte Saint-Denis, where Louis XIV is triumphantly crossing the Rhine. The Julien restaurant, on the right-hand side, was formerly a Parisian *bouillon*, like the Bouillon Chartier on the Rue du Faubourg-Montmartre, or the Bouillon Racine on the Rue Racine, where you could enjoy a bouillon of meat and vegetables. In the 1970s, it was still possible to eat very well here for next to nothing, but entrepreneurs who noticed its splendid Art Nouveau décor bought the building and have developed it into a fancy restaurant. Advertisements claim that you might meet Angelina Jolie or the French actor Fabrice Luchini here.

The Faubourg then crosses two parallel streets begun under Louis XVI and continued under Louis-Philippe, the Rue de l'Échiquier and the Rue d'Enghien. No. 10 on the Rue de l'Échiquier was the site of the Concert Layol, displaying the talents of Paulus, Yvette Gilbert and Dranem, then in later generations Lucienne Boyer, Marie Dubas, and even Raimu and Fernandel. On the same side, but in a different world, a Turkish-Kurdish bookstore bears the name Mevlana, who the owner tells me was a thirteenth-century mystic. As well as many religious works, you can also find here books on the Montessori method (in Turkish) or Che Guevara.

The crossroads of the Rue de l'Échiquier and the Rue d'Hauteville has a fine outlook, in one direction towards the monumental post office on the Rue du Faubourg-Poissonnière and the minaret of the Comptoir d'Escompte, in the other towards the church of Saint-Vincent-de-Paul, which encloses the Rue d'Hauteville and what remains of its Ashkenazi furriers in an impeccable stage set.

On the corner of the Rue d'Enghien and the Rue du Faubourg-Saint-Denis, the café Chez Jeannette has kept its fine 1950s décor almost intact. I frequented it when I used to train in a nearby boxing hall, whose décor and accessories had not changed since the era of Charles Rigoulot, the strongest man in the world, and the great Marcel Cerdan. Jeannette peeled vegetables for the evening meal with a nobility that I found very Parisian, without being entirely sure that she was not Breton or Picard. The young people who run the café today do not remember her.

'Fine 1950s décor' – since when did people start appreciating this style? When I was in my first year of medicine, in the frosty faculty on the Rue des Saints-Pères – this was 1955 – an old bistro on the corner of the Boulevard Saint-German was being refurbished, and we all found the new décor horrible. Today, Le Rouquet prides itself on its neon lights and Formica tops, its well-preserved '50s style'. We preferred at that time a café nearby, in a shack with a pointed roof on the corner of the Rue des Saint-Pères and the Rue Perronet. It was run by 'Père Mathieu', an old Auvergnat, who fed for free his student friends who came like him from the Massif Central, even paying for their books – which did not at all please his much younger wife, who saw her husband's consumption of alcohol and tobacco make away with their capital. Solidarity between Auvergnats was also expressed in higher realms: places as interns or externs were always found for natives of that province in the two major

neurology departments of the Salpêtrière, headed by emi-
nences who, with a background in Action Française or its
like, compensated by not accepting blacks or Jews.

The '30s style' that is also much admired today (even if
little represented in Paris outside of the 16th arrondissement) was despised by my parents and their friends. They
could not find words critical enough for the building on the
Rue Cassini where we lived – today a listed building, and
quite rightly so. It is as if each generation hates the architecture and design in which it spent its youth. This fluctuation
in taste is not specifically French. In Warsaw today, young
people enthuse over the Palace of Culture and Science, the
immense skyscraper from the 1950s that was a present from
the Soviet Union, and in comparison with which the Empire
State Building is a model of sobriety. Their parents detested
it as a symbol of both oppression and bad taste. Éditions
Hazan had a stand there at the book fair of 1990, when
it was expected that the post-communist countries would
become a big market. I remember old Poles who spent hours
browsing through our books, each of which probably cost
a month's salary for them, in sad contrast to the luxurious
interior of the building.

Will people one day find charm in Bofill's colonnades on
the Place de Catalogne, the bay windows in the Horloge
quarter, or the winds of the Avenue de France? We cannot
be sure. Each age has its good and its less good architecture.
Bernini found the dome of Val-de-Grâce 'a smallish skullcap
for a big head', and Ledoux made fun of the spindly columns of Gabriel's palaces on Place Louis-XV (today Place
de la Concorde).

A little after the Rue d'Enghien, the Cour des Petites-Écuries
opens onto the left-hand side of the Rue du Faubourg-
Saint-Denis. Fifty years ago this was the headquarters of the
leather merchants who lunched at the Brasserie Flo, where

service closed at nine o'clock in the evening. The cashier had a large wolfhound, and the place smelled of the black soap used to wash the wood floor. Flo and the whole court have changed a good deal, even becoming a kind of foreign island. Elegant young people sit at the terrace tables, and the pretty young girls in their entourage have nothing in common with the motley proletarian population around them.

At the far end of the court, a narrow passage leads to the Rue des Petites-Écuries, where a cultural centre run by Turkish Maoists is adorned with posters demanding the liberation of political prisoners in several Asian countries. A few metres away, the celebrity of the street is New Morning, a great spot for jazz in Paris since the 1980s, where such glories of the trumpet and saxophone as Chet Baker, Dizzy Gillespie, Archie Shepp and many others played.

Returning to the Rue du Faubourg-Saint-Denis, you cross the Rue de Paradis, the domain of porcelain and luxury glassware: Baccarat, Saint-Louis, Daum and Lalique have shops here, while the ancient Boulenger pottery even has a superb 1900 building whose front wall and column are topped by the curve of an immense glazed bay.

Before reaching the Boulevard Magenta, the Rue du Faubourg-Saint-Denis widens and opens to the left onto a rectangular park that serves to provide a little chlorophyll in this mineral quarter. Behind it, the façade of a chapel built under the Restoration by Louis-Pierre Baltard (the father of the 'Les Halles' Baltard) is the only remaining vestige of the immense hospital-prison of Saint-Lazare. In the 1630s, Vincent-de-Paul was given a former leper colony here to train missionaries, and the mission subsequently occupied an immense enclosure between the Faubourg-Saint-Denis and the Faubourg Poissonnière. Its main building served for various purposes over the centuries, all aimed at the repression of deviants: a house of correction under the Ancien Régime, where rebellious children were locked away; a prison for sexual criminals; a political prison at the time of the Revolution (André Chénier was sent to the scaffold from here); and still a prison in the nineteenth century, for loose women as well as for many Communards, including Louise Michel. In the 1930s, the building returned to its original role as a hospital: prostitutes affected with venereal disease were treated here; pox and clap were cared for before AIDS relegated them to second place in pathology. After being closed for a long while, the hospital was recently demolished to make way for the Françoise Sagan *mediathèque*. The new buildings, all white and echoing the arcades of the old hospital, have an almost Mediterranean aspect, unexpected but rather agreeable, and emphasized by the palm trees swaying in the courtyard.

The Rue du Faubourg-Saint-Denis continues across two major axes, first the Boulevard Magenta and then the Rue

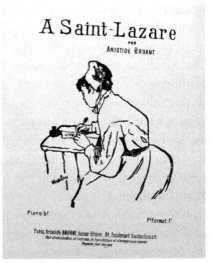

À Saint-Lazare, *Toulouse-Lautrec.*

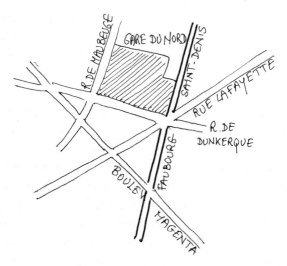

La Fayette: two enormous crossroads followed a little further by a third, where the two axes cross one another in front of the Gare du Nord.

The Boulevard Magenta and the Rue La Fayette each play the same role in the general design of the Right Bank: to join a central nerve centre – respectively the République and the Opéra – to the first slopes of the northern heights, Montmartre and Les Buttes-Chaumont. But despite this affinity in terms of town planning, the two axes are in no way similar. Any Parisian, whether by birth or adoption, and even any visitor, has the right to prefer whichever of the two they please. For my part, I sense the dynamic of the city by walking up the Rue La Fayette, whereas I avoid when possible the Boulevard Magenta. The former is the older of the two – originally known as Rue Charles X, which dates the start of this cutting. Finished much later – the bridge with concrete lattices that I referred to above dates from the 1930s – it has a great variety in terms of architecture, colour of stone, and the atmosphere of the quarters it crosses. There is nothing boring about the Rue La Fayette, whereas the Boulevard

Magenta aligns Haussmann and post-Haussmann buildings with a tiresome regularity. The height is the same from the Place de la République to Barbès: five storeys with a running balcony on the top floor, zinc roofs with skylights, dark grey stone, nothing to attract the eye. The views towards the stations, the Saint-Quentin market, and the porch of the Lariboisière hospital, are not enough to brighten up this long and falsely flat avenue, difficult for the cyclist, where the most numerous shops are agencies for temporary work.

Though many Parisians are unaware of it, the large esplanade in front of the Gare du Nord has been known since 1987 as the Place Napoléon-III. Very logically, the rehabilitation of Badinguet[4] began in that decade, when neoliberalism became unquestioned dogma. The shady adventurer, gang leader and author of the December massacre underwent a surreptitious mutation into the Saint-Simonian philanthropist, a pioneer of the modern banking and industrial system. This is why the municipal council, then presided over by Chirac, almost clandestinely gave Louis-Napoléon's name to a major Paris square. Perhaps there was already enough glorification of his victories in Italy – Magenta, Solférino, Turbigo – and Crimea – Alma, Malakoff, Sébastopol, Eupatoria. (We may note that no street celebrates the disastrous Mexican expedition. Even the battle of Camarón, a great deed of the Légion Étrangère, has no street in Paris.)

I said above that the façade of the Gare du Nord was a masterpiece. It is a shame that no one stops to contemplate it, whereas crowds throng in front of the façade of Notre-Dame, whose statuary is no older than that of the railway station. This façade has three storeys, their décor composed of fluted Doric columns and statues. Metal grilles have been installed between the columns implanted on the pavement, to prevent the homeless from protecting themselves from wind and rain. Higher up, on the middle level, statues of

Statues on the façade of the Gare du Nord.

northern cities alternate with columns – at the corners, the effigy of Douai on the Boulevard Magenta side, and that of Dunkirk on the side of the Rue du Faubourg-Saint-Denis. The upper level is a wide pediment supported by a curved arch and framed by colossal pillars. Its ascending stages culminate with a figure of Paris. On the sides, statues represent the northern capitals – Berlin, London, Brussels, Amsterdam. These proud and elegant women, dressed in the antique style, were sculpted by artists now forgotten, but are a match for many exhibited in the Musée d'Orsay.[5]

Despite its attractions, the Gare du Nord has hardly been an inspiration to writers or artists. In this field, the palm goes without contest to the Gare Saint-Lazare:

> those vast, glass-roofed sheds, like that of Saint-Lazare into which I went to find the train for Balbec, and which extended over the eviscerated city one of those bleak and boundless skies, heavy with an accumulation of dramatic menace, like certain skies painted with an almost Parisian

modernity by Mantegna or Veronese, beneath which only some terrible and solemn act could be in process, such as a departure by train or the erection of the Cross.[6]

Claude Monet devoted to these glass-roofed sheds a series of twelve canvases, and one of Édouard Manet's most famous paintings is often referred to as 'La Gare Saint-Lazare', even if this is only by allusion.[7] The difference in treatment received by these two stations is not hard to understand: when these painters and writers left Paris to take the air, they went to Normandy, to Balbec, to Giverny, to Honfleur, rather than to Maubeuge or Armentières. Many of them lived and worked close to the Gare Saint-Lazare – Mallarmé between the Lycée Condorcet and the Rue de Rome, Manet on the Rue d'Amsterdam, Caillebotte on the Boulevard Malesherbes.

The Gare du Nord is the last station whose surroundings still recall the destination of the trains that leave from here: 'À la Ville d'Aulnay', 'Au Rendez-Vous des Belges', 'La Tartine du Nord', 'À la Pinte du Nord' – only fast-food joints and Chinese restaurants escape this spell. The Gare Montparnasse, at the time of the famous photograph of a locomotive suspended in the void, was the centre of a Breton quarter in which Bécassine[8] could have felt at home. The construction of the Tour Montparnasse, the commercial centre and the new station has left only a scattering of *crêperies*. Around the Gare de Lyon there is scarcely any southern touch, though it is perhaps not accidental that the former Auvergnat quarter – the Rue de Lappe, the bottom of the Rue de la Roquette, where a dance hall, 'Au Massif central', occupied what are now the premises of the Théâtre de la Bastille – grew up around here.

Among the several brasseries opposite the Gare du Nord, the Terminus Nord used to be one of the most agreeable.

It then fell into the same hands and suffered the same fate as the Bouillon Julien I mentioned above, as well as Bofinger, La Coupole and Le Balzar: standardization of menus, impersonal reception, disappearance of those peculiarities that made each of these a meeting place with its regulars, its customs, its particular dishes. Out of all of these, it is the old Balzar that I miss the most – the others, in fact, I rarely went to, least of all La Coupole, too marked by memories of Sunday lunch there with my parents. But Le Balzar's celeriac remoulade, calf's head and breaded pig's feet were peerless, the waiters elegant and friendly, the globe lamps lit women in a radiant light, and sometimes, dining there after an operation that ran late, you might see Delphine Seyrig or Roger Blin coming out of the theatre. The passage of years may have embellished these souvenirs, but I could certainly find witnesses to confirm that Le Balzar was indeed an enchanting place.

The bulk of the Gare du Nord gives an impression of unity. The recent extension, set back and in a judiciously subdued architecture, does not disturb this. But this external

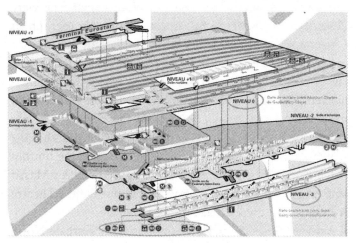

Levels of the Gare du Nord, diagram displayed in the station.

unity is a mask. Throughout its extent, the station is divided into three levels, one the same as the street and the others below. This demarcation is far more than simply spatial, as upper and lower no more communicate with one another than the world of the living and that of the shades did in the time of Ulysses.

The upper level is impeccable. Beneath the great glass roof the signs are clear, the seats are comfortable, a kiosk offers a choice of the foreign press, the cafés are clean and welcoming. This is where the Thalys trains leave for the northern capitals, as well as the Eurostar, protected by a security system like that of an airport. The travellers are executives, businessmen and women, tourists – white, clean, and well-dressed.

Going down, level -1 is no worse than the Châtelet station of the RER. It is the vast level -2 that needs to be seen. The ceiling is low, the colours dark, the lighting dim, the signs incomprehensible and the announcements inaudible. As there are more than forty suburban train lines, the result is a gloomy labyrinth. Those who arrive every morning and leave every evening, from Goussainville, Luzarches, Persan-Beaumont or Villiers-le-Bel, know where they are, but all others wander across the platforms looking for the train to take them to the Châtelet or out to Roissy. The population on this lower level are in great majority black. The videos taken during the station's periodic riots show angry black crowds, yet only a few Arabs, which illuminates the difference between the two populations. The blacks, more recent arrivals and hence more fragile in status, are pushed out miles from anywhere, whereas the Arabs are well settled in the communes of the inner suburbs, Saint-Denis, Aubervilliers, Gennevilliers, accessible by Métro. As for the whites here, they are haggard tourists trying to decipher announcements as mysterious as ancient oracles, and muscular railway police whose brutality is well known to the 'users'.

It is impossible to attempt here what Anna Maria Ortese admirably succeeded in doing in her *Silenzio a Milano*[9] – spend the night on a bench observing the humanity that chooses a railway station as refuge amid the brutality of life. Impossible because there are no benches here.

Once you pass the station, the first remarkable point on the Rue du Faubourg-Saint-Denis is the Fernand-Widal hospital, which until 1959 was known by everyone under the name of Maison Dubois. Antoine Dubois was a great surgeon under the Empire and the Restoration, consultant to Napoleon, obstetrician to Empress Marie-Louise and later to the Duchesse de Berry. He was director of a clinic on the Rue du Faubourg-Saint-Martin, which moved to its present site after his death but kept his name on account of his great popularity in Paris – he also has a street named after him between the Rue de l'École-de-Médicine and the Rue Monsieur-le-Prince. The Maison Dubois was a paying establishment. In a letter to Ancelle, his family's lawyer, Baudelaire, arranging for his mistress, Jeanne Duval, to be hospitalized there, wrote:

On 3 May [1859] I have to pay 120 francs to the clinic plus 30 francs for care. I cannot go to Paris [he was at Honfleur]. Use the Saturday (tomorrow) to have my mother cash the enclosed bill, and on Sunday send 150 francs (a 100 franc note and a 50) or a money order to M. le Directeur de la Maison municipal de santé, 200 faubourg Saint-Denis. You can say in your letter that you are sending this on behalf of M. Baudelaire for the stay of Mlle Jeanne Duval, that there is 120 francs for her stay and the 30 francs are to be handed to the patient herself for her care.

The Maison Dubois saw many writers and artists pass through its doors, including Nerval, on the occasion of one of his crises towards the end of his life, and Murger, who died there in 1861.

The front side that faces the boulevard is in no way remarkable, but the inner courtyards – designed by Théodore Labrouste, younger brother of Henri Labrouste, the architect of the Sainte-Geneviève library and the reading room of the Bibliothèque Nationale – are pleasant, the first courtyard surrounded by arcades supported by colonnades, the second planted with an avenue of maples. A younger brother's architecture, modest and well-groomed.

It was in the Maison Dubois that I first joined the working life of a hospital. This was on the lowest rung of the ladder ('performing an extern's function'), but this tiny step was a qualitative leap. I found myself admitted into a territory peopled by characters of a different nature, dressed in the white coat provided by the hospital and fastened by toggles, instead of the apprentice's coat washed at home, as well as the perspective of earning a few francs at the end of the month. It was intoxicating.

The surgical unit where I practised my minuscule functions was presided over by a disciple of Mondor, Professor Olivier: parting in the middle, half-moon glasses, bow tie, unfailing arrogance – the typical surgeon of that time. Fortunately he had assistants who struck me as well-meaning and went so far as to call me by my name, naturally in the polite '*vous*' – the familiar '*tu*' would only come when you passed the internship examination, a simple but decisive sign of your admission to their caste. This (and the history of the French Revolution) is very likely why I acquired the habit of calling everyone '*tu*', except those whom I know will not reply in the same way.

The patients in this hospital were poor people from

around the railway stations, French proletarians and immigrants from Italy, Spain, North Africa. The quarter was black and dirty with the smoke of the trains. Electrification had only just begun. This was the time when second-class carriages were decorated with black-and-white photographs of Bagnères-de-Bigorre, Berck-Plage or Autun, when one of the railway staff would strike the carriage wheels with a long-handled hammer to detect possible cracks, and when trains to the south stopped at Laroche-Migennes to 'take on water'. (Evoking these images, I think of my father likewise relating memories of another time – that his teachers wore frock coats to their lectures, that it took five days to reach France from his native Egypt, and that bets were laid each night on the number of miles travelled that day.)

The faubourg had a 'bad reputation', as people would say in those days. I remember an emergency admission of a man with a bullet in his stomach, probably the stomach wall as he could still walk. He asked for the bullet to be removed, but refused to be registered and admitted. When it was explained to him that this was not possible, he left just as he had arrived.

We have to fear that the Assistance Publique, in its concern for profitability and standardization, will one day close this small hospital, as it has closed Boucicaut, where the nurses were still nuns when I was an intern there, the Vaugirard hospital with its fine gardens, the Saint-Vincent-de-Paul where Gilbert Huault worked, the Broca close to Boulevard Arago which specialized in skin diseases, the Bretonneau that took in poor children from Montmartre, and the Laennec, where I worked for some twenty years. It is true that these establishments were not 'rational'. At Laennec, for example, there was a heart surgery unit – my own – but not a cardiology department; the technical level (not a phrase used) was rudimentary, and patients had to be sent all over Paris to have their eyes or their knees treated. But these small hospitals could have been improved to meet local needs instead of destroying them, selling their land to developers and replacing them with monsters like the Georges-Pompidou hospital where, as if it was not enough to be ill, you are immersed in an atmosphere that varies over the course of the day between that of an airport and that of a modern prison. Whereas the destroyed hospitals animated their area with the presence of students, nurses, visitors, the surroundings of the Pompidou hospital are more like the downtown of Phoenix, Arizona. One night I actually got lost there, and could not find anyone to show me the way back.

From the Fernand-Widal hospital to the Place de la Chapelle, the Rue du Faubourg-Saint-Denis is the hub of an Asian quarter that grew up a good twenty years ago and today stretches into the adjacent streets – Cail, Louis-Blanc, Perdonnet. In colourful shops, amid the rich smell of spices, you can buy jewellery from junk to fine gold, saris, Bollywood films, ginger, guavas, and many other fruit that I can't identify. Parisians often call this quarter 'Indian' or even 'Pakistani', but if there are certainly Hindi-speaking Indians as well as natives of Pakistan or Bangladesh here, the majority are Tamils. Some come from south-east India, the state of Tamil Nadu ('land of the Tamils'), whose largest city is Madras. Others are Sri Lankan – perhaps they supported the independence war of the Tamil Tigers, preserving this memory after the horrific massacres by the island's central government.

This fragment of Asia is one of the Parisian quarters sometimes referred to as 'ethnic', a word imported from America, where it means something more like exotic ('ethnic restaurant', 'ethnic dress'), whereas in the French version the notion of race is scarcely concealed. Each of these quarters has its history, with highs and lows that may even lead to its complete disappearance, whether by assimilation or repatriation. I remember for example the extinction of the white Russian colony around the Avenue de Versailles. Few still remember that a Russian newspaper used to appear each week in the postwar years, for which M. Dominique, who ran a famous restaurant on the Rue Bréa in Montparnasse, wrote the theatre notes. The Spanish flavour that the Avenue de Wagram had in Franco's last years – a time when the Parisian bourgeoisie had maids and buildings had concierges – has also disappeared, as well as the Japanese enclave along the Rues Sainte-Anne and Petits-Champs, leaving only a few gastronomic addresses.

But neither Russians nor Spaniards nor Japanese were numerous enough in Paris to form genuine quarters. On the other hand, the old Jewish quarter still exists in and around the Rue des Rosiers, though it is threatened on all sides. The Yiddish-Ashkenazi part of its population, overwhelming in the days when the Rue Ferdinand-Duval was known as the Jewish street, has gradually aged and disappeared. On the site of Goldenberg's grocery, where I often went on Sunday mornings with my father to buy *pickelfleisch* and *malossols*, and where Jo Goldenberg greeted his customers with a broad Parisian accent unlikely in such a place, there is today a Japanese clothes shop. The quarter is experiencing converging and even combined pressures, that of gay bars and that of fashion, which are steadily gaining ground on the Rue des Rosiers and nearby, where the street names – Blancs-Manteaux, Guillemites, Hospitalières-Saint-Gervais – come straight from the Middle Ages and remind us of the religious congregations that at one time shared this region.

The Arab Goutte-d'Or, the African quarter of the Dejean market, is also under a double threat, the omnipresent one of the police and that of a gentrification that is visibly progressing, the two being as closely tied as the fingers of one hand, or as profit and violence if you prefer. By comparison, the two Chinatowns, that of the 13th arrondissement and the smaller though older one of Belleville, are prosperous and peaceful, and steadily expanding on their margins. The Chinese have even managed to create their own Sentier in the old Rues Popincourt and Sedaine, from which any trace of urban life has now disappeared under the implacable monotony of ready-to-wear. This little quarter, which was the centre of Protestantism in Paris at the time of the Reformation, before becoming par excellence the site of barricades in the nineteenth century, is now very sad. On the other hand, we can only rejoice that many *tabacs* have been taken over by Chinese, far more efficient than their traditional grumpy proprietors.

CHAPTER 7

The long, fascinating and magnificent Rue du Faubourg-Saint-Denis ends at the Place de la Chapelle: a halt as at the threshold to another world. You are facing what was one of the great gates in the Wall of the Farmers-General, today traced by the overhead Métro. (The engineers for the Métro line chose the space freed by the destruction of the wall in the 1860s as suitable for this great project.)

At the start of my journey, I crossed the Wall of the Farmers-General to enter the city at the Barrière d'Italie, but there is no symmetry here. The wall was more substantial to the north than to the south, where in some places it had not yet been completed on the eve of the Revolution, the gaps being closed by palisades or simply wooden boards. This was because goods subject to excise duty at the gates – wine, wheat and wood – arrived more from the north and east of the city than from the south. There are still signs of this in present-day Paris, where, in the bourgeois quarters and on the Left Bank, the roads that follow the line of the old wall, like the Avenue Kléber or the Boulevard Raspail, have two symmetrical sides, whereas in the north and east the inner and outer sides often remain different, creating a persisting border effect.

What would you find beyond this gate before the destruction of the wall, before the Paris boundary extended to the fortifications (the present-day Boulevards des Maréchaux)? One commune, La Chapelle-Saint-Denis, was arranged on a north-south axis along the 'La Chapelle highway' – today the Rue Marx-Dormoy then the Rue de la Chapelle. Until the 1840s this was still countryside, with vineyards (La Goutte d'Or was a white wine whose reputation went back to Henri IV), windmills, gypsum quarries and highway bars.[1] The main market for dairy cattle in the Paris region was held here.

But far more than its neighbours – Montmartre on one side, La Villette on the other – La Chapelle-Saint-Denis would be transformed by the railway. The northern and eastern railways were built on its territory, occupying large expanses and chasing the vineyards and game a long way away. In ten years the commune became industrial, with workshops and warehouses, locomotive and steam-engine works, cloth printing, chemical plants, salt and sugar refineries. The population was then working-class. After the revolution of February 1848, the great works on the railway became National Workshops, with the result that in the course of the June Days (which were triggered by the closing of these workshops) the national guard of La Chapelle-Saint-Denis went over to the side of the insurrection – one of its lieutenants, Legénissel, an industrial designer, commanding the barricades on the Rue La Fayette at the corner with the Rue d'Abbeville, and giving Lamoricière's troops a great deal of trouble.[2]

Railway tracks still mark the landscape of the 18th arrondissement, but those from the Gare du Nord and the Gare de l'Est are not embedded in the urban fabric the same way. The latter are bordered by streets – the Rue d'Alsace, the Rue Philippe-de-Girard, the Rue d'Aubervilliers – which include them in the landscape. The former, in contrast, are bordered by buildings that turn their backs to them, standing almost vertically above the rails. It is only possible to see the tracks, therefore, from the bridges that span them – provided that these open skies and vistas of the banlieue are

*Rue Stephenson, building above the
railway from the Gare du Nord.*

preserved, and the town-planners and developers do not get
the idea into their heads of gaining new space by covering
over the tracks as at the Gare d'Austerlitz.

In contrast to Barbès, the Place de la Chapelle is not a
crossroads dislocated and crushed by the overhead Métro.
Here, the two sides of the Boulevard de la Chapelle diverge,
and the space between them forms a little park. Its corners
are occupied by three cafés (one of these a 'Danton', which
must date from the centenary of 1789, like the statue at
the Odéon crossroads), and the fine theatre of Les Bouffes-
du-Nord. The Métro station is not located in the middle of
the intersection as at Barbès – the parallel between these
two neighbours, both crossed by the railway, is evident
– but shifted some twenty metres further east (towards
Stalingrad), allowing us to see the impeccable design of the
external stairway, the care taken to connect it to the glass

panels of the platform, and the bridge with its high stone pillars that support the ensemble.

The two scraggy parks between the Métro and the left side of the street have plane trees that provide shade in summer. (At the time I passed here, the one on the left – looking outward – served as an encampment for refugees, who had settled or resettled here after the police violence on the Rue Pajol.) The newspaper kiosk, against the park on the right, was formerly run by a young woman who was Arab, Trotskyist, and veiled, which is not so common. In brief, if the Place de la Chapelle can be seen, and is often seen, as a site of noise, dirt and giant traffic jams, you can also – as I do – find poetry here, and even a certain gentleness. (This is my only use of the word 'poetry' in this book, I promise.)

The major road that crosses the Place de la Chapelle in an almost straight line initially bears the name of Marx Dormoy, the socialist interior minister in 1937 following the suicide of Roger Salengro. (Dormoy was himself murdered in 1941 by the Cagoule, which he had not succeeded in eradicating.) This is bordered by bourgeois buildings from the late nineteenth century, by the cheap housing of a working-class banlieue, much of which is walled off, and by 1960s constructions set considerably back, which emphasizes their ugliness. (It is scarcely conceivable that we had to wait until 1977 for new buildings to be no longer set back in this way. The law that prescribed alignment dated from the Empire, and had the aim – though not the effect – of leading in time to a widening of the roads.) The population here are Arab and black (there are very few Tamils in the 18th arrondissement), poor as are the shops and cafés, not to mention the people who ask you for a cigarette. The Rue Marx-Dormoy, and still more so the Rue de la Chapelle that continues it, is a proletarian street, similar to the

Rue d'Avron in the 20th arrondissement – which also runs between a former gate in the Wall of the Farmers-General (the Barrière de Montreuil) and the shambles of the Porte de Montreuil.

Soon after crossing the Rue Ordener and the Rue Riquet, the church of Saint-Denis-de-la-Chapelle and the basilica of Sainte-Jeanne-d'Arc form on the right-hand pavement a massive Catholic presence that is unexpected in such a place. These two elements, different in all respects, are united by the figure of Jeanne d'Arc, a bronze statue of whom gives life to façades that are not very welcoming. In front of this statue, a Belgian tourist who collects photos of his heroine asks me if I know of any others in Paris, apart from the one on the Rue des Pyramides that he has just visited. I tell him of those on the Rue Jeanne-d'Arc, on the esplanade of the Sacré-Coeur and the parvis of Saint-Augustin, as well as the helmeted one on the Rue Saint-Honoré, which recalls how Jeanne was wounded there by an English arrow. It was just before she led a charge against the English that she is said to have meditated here, in the church of Saint-Denis – of which almost nothing medieval remains, apart from a few capitals of the right-hand span.

The history of the adjoining basilica is a curious one. In September 1914, when Paris was threatened by the German advance, the archbishop solemnly pronounced in front of Notre-Dame the vow to erect a basilica consecrated to Jeanne d'Arc if the city was saved. After the war, the project was put into execution. Sadly, the municipal authorities rejected a design by Auguste Perre for a concrete tower 200 metres tall, which he would construct thirty years later at Le Havre. The actual construction, finished in the 1950s, has a fortress-like exterior and the interior of a concrete icebox. To see any quantity of white people in this quarter, you need to come here on Sunday at the time of mass.

The urban fabric then steadily unravels until you reach the Porte de la Chapelle, where it gives way to an inextricable jumble of slip roads to the motorways and the Périphérique, railways in every direction, and the inaccessible tiny green spaces that I mentioned at the start of this journey. Just before this, to the left, an enormous construction site alongside the railway from the Gare du Nord is named 'Chapelle International'. On the corner with the Boulevard Ney, a billboard gives the details of a 'programme unprecedented in France', christened SOHO (Small Office, Home Office): 'To bring together activity spaces and residential spaces in a single project', establishing 'a lasting cohabitation between city and railway'. The images of this synthesis are frightening.

La Chapelle is divided in two both by its major north-south axis and by the railway from the Gare du Nord. On the Boulevard Barbès side, as far as the very old Rue des Poissonniers, which is where seafood arrived in Paris from Boulogne before the building of the railway, you have La

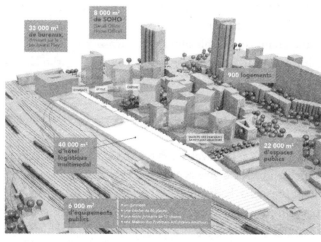

Boulevard Ney, billboard for the Chapelle International project.

Goutte-d'Or. This extends beyond the Rue Myrha (named after the daughter of a mayor of Montmartre, rather than Myrrha, daughter of the king of Cyprus whose tribulations Ovid relates in his *Metamorphoses*) up to the Porte des Poissonniers, a quarter that is nameless but not without character. On the other side, to the east as far as the Rue d'Aubervilliers, is a zone now rapidly changing, where on each visit you find new depredations. Communication between these two halves of La Chapelle is reduced, as there are only three bridges where the railway can be crossed, on the Rue de Jessaint, the Rue Doudeauville and the Rue Ordener. The two regions thus remain different in every respect, and even foreign to one another.

For a long time, La Goutte d'Or was a foothill of Montmartre, a hill where gypsum was extracted, partly open-cast and partly in quarries such as the one Nerval evokes in *October Nights*, which 'resembled a Druidic temple with its tall pillars supporting square-shaped vaults. You looked down into its depths, almost afraid that the awesome gods of our ancestors – Esus, Thoth or Cernunnos – would emerge into view.'[3] On the surface, between the vines, five windmills used to turn at the mouths of the ovens to mill plaster, an indispensable material in 'this illustrious valley of rubble constantly close to falling, and of streams black with mud', as Balzac writes at the start of *Old Goriot*.

As far as the present Goutte-d'Or is concerned, a kind of confusion or superposition is often made between it and Barbès. It is true that La Goutte-d'Or is bordered on two of its sides by the Boulevard Barbès and the Boulevard de la Chapelle, but these are borders that might be called external. Barbès is a bazaar in the original sense of the term: everything can be found here, which is not the case with La Goutte-d'Or. At the start of the present century, I lived on the Rue de Sofia, a small side street that comes out into

Plaster quarries of La Goutte-d'Or,
late nineteenth-century engraving.

the Boulevard Barbès opposite the Rue de la Goutte-d'Or. In the dozen or so years since then, the things sold in the bazaar have changed a bit: suitcases are slower to move, mobile phones much quicker, while jewellery and cut-price goods go much the same. The most striking development is the gentrification of Barbès, which is far more marked than that of La Goutte-d'Or. Its most obvious signs are the renovation of the Le Louxor cinema (which it would be foolish to complain about), and above all the establishment of a luxury brasserie on the corner of Boulevard Barbès and Boulevard de la Chapelle. Implanted on the site of a cut-price goods store that burned down – its ruins were used as a platform at the time of the banned demonstration against Israeli intervention in Gaza in July 2014 – this establishment is not only an offence to the spirit of the place, but also a kind of test: how far can you go before 'those people' start to break everything?

I do not know when La Goutte-d'Or became the quarter of Paris's Arab wholesalers, and Barbès a bazaar for suitcases and contraband cigarettes. What is certain is that the Algerians who settled here made a bad choice, the district having now been for a long time one of the poorest and most neglected in the city. It was so even before the cutting of the Boulevard Barbès and the Boulevard Magenta shifted the old crossroads, in the days when the Rue des Poissonniers and the Rue du Faubourg-Poissonnière met at the *barrière*, when, at the start of Zola's *L'Assommoir*, Gervaise's eyes 'persistently returned to the Barrière Poissonnière, watching dully the uninterrupted flow of men and cattle, wagons and sheep, which came down from Montmartre and from La Chapelle'. From her window in the Hôtel Boncoeur ('on the Boulevard de la Chapelle, at the left of the Barrière Poissonnière, a two-storey building, painted a deep red up to the first floor, with disjointed weather-stained blinds'), she looks out into the night for the return of her lover, Lantier:

> She looked to the right toward the Boulevard de Rochechouart, where groups of butchers stood with their bloody frocks before their establishments, and the fresh breeze brought in whiffs, a strong animal smell – the smell of slaughtered cattle. She looked to the left, following the ribbon-like avenue, past the Lariboisière hospital, then being built. Slowly, from one end to the other of the horizon, did she follow the wall, from behind which in the night-time she had heard strange groans and cries, as if some fell murder were being perpetrated. She looked at it with horror, as if in some dark corner – dark with dampness and filth – she should distinguish Lantier – Lantier lying dead with his throat cut.

A magnificent passage, which sets the date of the narrative. The Hôpital du Nord acquired its present name when the Comtesse Lariboisière financed the completion of the works, around 1850. The last shots of the June Days of 1848 were fired on the construction site, where Coupeau, Gervaise's new lover, worked as a plumber. I think of all this in seeing the landscape pass between La Chapelle and Barbès, against the characteristic metallic scraping sound of the overhead Métro. It seemed to me at one time that Zola exaggerated, that from a second storey on the Boulevard de la Chapelle you could not see at the same time both the hospital and the slaughterhouses (where the park on the Place d'Anvers is now). But checking from the discount store, Tati, he was right.

Some more here about those June Days. The street outside the façade of the Saint-Bernard church in La Goutte-d'Or is the Rue Affre, after the archbishop of Paris killed at this time. The street adjacent to the Saint-Joseph church, on the Rue Saint-Maur, is named after Monsignor Darboy, another archbishop, shot during the first week of the Commune. The first of these streets is close to Lariboisière and the second to Père-Lachaise, both places where insurgents were massacred in the final hours of these events. By remembering these dignitaries of the church in such working-class districts, the notables of the Third Republic probably sought to bring home to the survivors and their descendants the full horror of these crimes, and to spell out what would await them in the case of recidivism.

I owe my knowledge of La Goutte-d'Or to the last authentic representative of Belgian surrealism, Maurice Culot. It was he who introduced me to this quarter in 1984, when he was working on his great book on the subject.[4] He showed me the traces of streets in a St Andrew's cross (a flattened 'X'), creating gentle slopes, dispensing with steps, and giving buildings on street corners a bevelled edge – particularly noticeable at the corner of Rue de Chartres and Rue de la Charbonnière. He took me around all the sites of *L'Assommoir*, which were already demolished or in the process of demolition – the café of Old Colombe that gave its name to the book, the Rue des Islettes where Zola located both Gervaise's home and the washhouse where she worked. Above all, he explained to me the absurdity of the development now under way, the thin concrete colonnades, the unnatural levelling of the hill, the faults of alignment, the amputation of acute angles. Nothing has been settled since that time. A police station has been implanted in the middle of the Rue de la Goutte-d'Or, reputedly one of the most brutal in Paris. The Rue des Islettes has been ravaged, and is now bordered on one side by a hideous primary school above an underground car park, and on the other by a post office in front of which is a wasteland that, with consummate if involuntary irony, has been given the name 'Place de l'Assomoir'. The mosque, on the corner of Rue Polonceau and Rue des Poissonniers, was demolished in 2013. There is a plan to build on this site an Institut des Cultures d'Islam, which will probably be as deserted as the one that already exists on the Rue Stephenson. Between the Rue de la Goutte-d'Or and the Rue Polonceau, a gloomy stairway has been constructed and named after Boris Vian. Poor Boris; what sins did he have to expiate to be given this place out of thousands of others? On the Rue des Gardes, the Paris municipality has implanted a row of fashion shops, 'creators' for whom the term 'out of place' would be insufficient; 'obscene' is a better term. Not that the poor are not entitled to dress themselves nicely – but to exhibit dresses worth a fortune in such a place!

So, is there still any reason to visit La Goutte-d'Or? Yes indeed, as it has, like the Noailles market in Marseille, the

Rue Polonceau, poster on the site of the demolished mosque.

atmosphere of an Arab city with its liveliness, the smell of spices, the warm reception, the gentleness – regarding this word, which goes against everything that is said and written at the moment, I recall an event that dates from the time when I lived on the Rue de Sofia. One Sunday morning, I was walking with my daughter Cléo, then two years old in a pushchair, when an old Algerian came up to me on the Rue de Chartres, leaned down and kissed her hand. That sums up the whole charm of La Goutte-d'Or.

It was with *L'Assommoir* that Zola made his entry as one of the great writers of Paris, all of whom were in their way walkers. Zola himself walked with pencil and notebook in his hand, taking notes and making sketches. Balzac ran right across Paris, between his printers, his coffee dealers, his visits to houses to find a dwelling for 'the Foreigner', Madame Hanska. Sometimes he walked at random, scrutinizing shop signs in search of the name for a character (I have quoted elsewhere the passage in which Gozlan tells

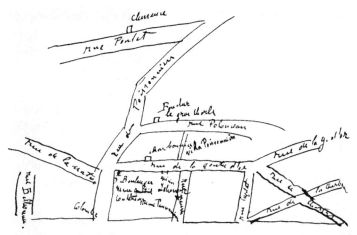

Sketch by Émile Zola, made during the preparation of L'Assommoir.

how he was dragged, exhausted, through the 'Rues du Mail, de Cléry, du Cardan, du Faubourg-Montmartre . . . and the Place des Victoires', until on the Rue du Bouloi, Balzac finally found what he was looking for: 'Marcas! What do you think? Marcas! What a name! Marcas!'[5]). Was this also how, by walking, he found names so fitting that they became types: Nucingen, Rastignac, Gobseck, Birotteau? As for Baudelaire, who had nothing at home – when he did have a home – it was in the street that he worked. He says as much at the start of his poem 'Sun':

> I go alone to try my fanciful fencing,
> Scenting in every corner the chance of a rhyme,
> Stumbling over words as over paving stones,
> Colliding at times with lines dreamed of long ago.

In the twentieth century, those for whom Paris is not a back-cloth but a theme, from Carco to Breton, Calet to Debord, have also been great walkers. Proust is a special case: he did not stroll through the city, perhaps on account of his 'suffocations', perhaps because it was not his subject. Apart from the gardens of the Champs-Élysées and the Bois, he describes it only rarely. The passages from *The Captive*, when he gives us notes on the city as precious as on some Norman church, are drawn from the moment of awakening, in the bedroom where the shutters are still closed. There are sounds which make it possible to divine what the weather will be ('according to whether they came to my ears deadened and distorted by the moisture of the atmosphere or quivering like arrows in the resonant, empty expanses of a spacious, frosty, pure morning; as soon as I heard the rumble of the first tramcar, I could tell whether it was sodden with rain or setting forth into the blue'); or else the cries of street sellers, such as the snail merchant:

> For after having almost 'spoken' the refrain: 'Who'll buy my snails, fine, fresh snails?' it was with the vague sadness of Maeterlinck, transposed into music by Debussy, that the snail vendor, in one of those mournful cadences in which the composer of *Pelléas* shows his kinship with Rameau: 'If vanquished I must be, is it for thee to be my vanquisher?' added with a singsong melancholy: 'Only tuppence a dozen.'[6]

After this passage, all the more digressive in that Proust had probably never heard anyone mention La Goutte-d'Or, unless he had read *L'Assommoir*, I cross the Rue Myrha and enter a different quarter. Rue Doudeauville, Rue de Panama, Rue de Suez, the colours of fabrics, the hairdressers, the restaurants, the wholesalers offering fresh produce from Congo-Kinshasa, the market on the Rue Dejean where you can find all the fish of the Gulf of Guinea (Nile perch, tilapia, thiof, sompate, *plas-plas*). This is a corner of Africa, different from the Rue du Château-d'Eau and its hairdressers, but just as animated and joyful. Crossing from one world into another, at the corner of the Rue Labat, my thoughts turned to Sarah Kofman, a philosopher who wrote the finest book on the life of Jews in Paris under the Occupation, *Rue Ordener, rue Labat* – the finest along with *Quoi de neuf sur la guerre?* by Robert Bober, which takes place around the Cirque d'Hiver.[7]

Continuing on the Rue des Poissonniers after the Rue Ordener and the Marcadet-Poissonniers Métro station, I pass into a 'normal' and rather unpleasant quarter. In the past it was saved by the view over the roofs of the repair workshops of the railways from the Gare du Nord, humped like the backs of prehistoric animals. These workshops have disappeared. Where are sick locomotives repaired today? Perhaps the very idea of repair as we used to understand it is obsolete, and a technician with a computer notes a defective sensor which is replaced in two minutes. And with something more serious, such as an axle, a problem with the suspension, the engine is just left to rot in a corner. On the site of these workshops, in any case, there are now large buildings that block the view, storage spaces and food wholesalers. This side of the Rue des Poissonniers is a place where one day students of architecture will be shown how far commercial vulgarity and tack could go in our age.

There is however a reason to make the journey to this remote corner, as it contains, almost hidden, one of the finest Paris constructions of the twentieth century: the Henri Sauvage building on the Rue des Amiraux (a name given in homage to the role of the navy in the defence of Paris in 1871). This is more than a building: a rectangular block clad with white tiles, a tall succession of stepped terraces, corners rounded into quasi-towers, openings arranged in a rigorous variety, a perfect symmetry between the two sides, in short, a miracle of invention and grace. To the side is an indoor swimming pool, entered beneath an exquisitely designed glass canopy on which a few touches of blue tiling accentuate the overall whiteness. This masterpiece is as good as the building also designed by Sauvage on the Rue Vavin, which is better known, since Montparnasse is more visited. It is a great shame that Sauvage's plan for the Porte Maillot was not accepted – two immense stepped pyramids that would have framed the entrance that the west of Paris lacked.

The Rue des Poissonniers ends up at the *porte* of the same name, which is what Marc Augé – my friend at the Lycée Louis-le-Grand for several years before going on to become a famous ethnologist – would call a non-place.

To head north from the Place de la Chapelle, I could take a different route, zigzagging between the Marx-Dormoy–La Chapelle axis and the railway from the Gare de l'Est through the Rue Pajol, which leads to a micro-quarter centred on the market on the Rue d'Olive (named after the first governor of Mauritius). A few years ago, the covered markets

Henri Sauvage's plan for the Porte Maillot, 1931.

of Paris were the object of an offensive by the municipal authorities that aimed to make them into 'cultural spaces', 'sports spaces', 'gastronomic spaces' or the like. After the Enfants-Rouge – one of the last places where you hear Yiddish spoken in Paris, which has been totally denatured if not destroyed – the Secrétan market, and the ancient Carreau du Temple, which you could believe was forever devoted to leather and velvet, likewise saw their metal and glass structures ravaged, and their activities, so useful and Parisian, become those of the mall of a small American town. The Rue d'Olive market has happily preserved its buildings and its original activity. The streets around it are calm, bordered by the working-class housing of the nineteenth century that is the connective tissue of La Chapelle. In other words, this is 'an agreeable corner', and as is usual in such cases, subject to a process of embourgeoisement – a term rather more accurate than 'gentrification', as there are no signs that 'gentry' have anything to do with this typically petty-bourgeois phenomenon.

Here this process is still in its beginnings. The context has not changed, just the population. Alongside the Chinese, Arabs, and poor people from all origins who still populated this quarter ten years ago, young white people have now moved in – not that well off, but as sophisticated as in Belleville or Aligre, with their dress codes, pushchairs, trainers, hairstyles and iPads. We know the rest from having seen it appear and spread in Bastille, Oberkampf, Gambetta, Rue Montorgeuil, along the Canal Saint-Martin. Cafés proliferate, become restaurants, and on sunny days their terraces spread together in a seamless tablecloth, hosting young people so uniform that they might be cloned. Organic groceries are opened, delicatessens, Japanese restaurants. Then the old shops, shoe repairers, stationers or Arab patisseries, lower their shutters, and when these reopen, they are transformed into art galleries. Behind the works exhibited, files are stacked on shelves and young people tap on their computers. No one enters or leaves, no one stops to look, it's a sign of the death throes of a working-class neighbourhood.

As a petit-bourgeois who has lived for over thirty years in quarters that have been gentrified one after the other, I can appreciate the contradiction in describing critically a phenomenon that, whether I willed it or not, I ended up being involved in. You would have to move home periodically, or settle a long way out, to avoid this threat for good and all.

Starting from the Rue d'Olive market, the Rue de l'Évangile leads towards the star of the Place Hébert (after a former mayor, and not the ever unjustly slandered Père Duchesne). It then describes a long curve between the railways from the Gare de l'Est on the right, and on the left the enormous Cap 18, a business park for small companies – photogravure, printing, cabling, carpentry, glass works – under an architecture that has the merit of a low profile. Until the late 1950s, this space was occupied by a tight cluster of gasometers, tall black cylinders often photographed by the big names of the time.

Where the Rue de l'Évangile comes out into Rue d'Aubervilliers there is a *calvaire* that gave its name to the 'Rue du Calvaire-de-l'Évangile'. This street disappeared long ago, but the large bronze Christ is still there, more exotic in the modern landscape than it was against the backdrop of the gasometers. I had stopped in front of the statue when an old man in a djellaba, wearing the flat cap of pious Muslims, deposited on its plinth two candles contained in those small aluminium holders sold in supermarkets and churches, and proceeded to light them. Turning round, he saw my surprise and said to me softly: 'I believe in all the gods, all the gods are good and just.' And this polytheist hobbled off on his way.

Reaching the Rue d'Aubervilliers, I was lost for a moment. I no longer knew where I was, unable to recognize the familiar Porte d'Aubervilliers, a little roundabout where, as I remember, the Boulevard Ney continued without a break into the Boulevard Macdonald. Straight ahead, instead of the narrow Avenue de la Porte-d'Aubervilliers was a wide road bordered by recent new buildings. In particular, to my right, what I finally identified as the Boulevard Macdonald was quite new and amazing. Hoardings explained this apparition: the Calberson warehouses, which since had the 1960s stretched between the Porte de la Chapelle and the Porte de la Villette, have been completely transformed in this segment of the boulevard – transfigured and transmuted.

It was the Office for Metropolitan Architecture (OMA), the agency of Rem Koolhaas, that took charge of this major project. Its idea was to keep the footprint of the old warehouses, with an interrupted motif for more than 600 metres in the form of a metallic grille between two bands

© René-Jacques. Ministère de la Culture–Médiathèque du Patrimonie/Archives d'architecture du XXe siècle

Gasometers and calvary, Rue d'Aubervilliers.

of concrete, at what would normally be the second-floor level. Even at its only break, in the middle of the block, the pattern continues as a bridge above the tramlines. Aligned on this basis are modules designed by each of the project's fifteen architects. The first level, less high than the others, is set back, so that the modules are slightly cantilevered. They are joined together, aligned and of the same height, but the design, the width and the colour are different. Some of them are offices, others housing, others again storage units. The design was given freer rein at the two ends: facing the Porte d'Aubervilliers, the Portzamparc module is distinguished by its orange colour and the stilts on which it rests; towards the Porte de la Villette, where all the public services are congregated – school, college, sports hall – the Kengo Kuma agency designed opposite the Canal Saint-Denis a large module to which an asymmetrical double-sloped roof, and an oblique salient above windows like two round eyes, give a Japanese touch. This feat of urbanism may lack imagination, but all the same, the ensemble is superior to anything else built today in this sector.

Opposite, between the Boulevard Macdonald and the Périphérique, on the site where the Claude-Bernard hospital was demolished in the 1990s, a new quarter is being constructed, in which certain buildings are debatable – the cinema and the school in particular – but which as a whole is well articulated and avoids the mistakes committed beside the Bibliothèque de France, where wide avenues are open to the winds. The Périphérique itself, bordered by an anti-noise barrier and a clump of trees, is crossed by a pedestrian bridge leading to Aubervilliers – the gleaming summit of Le Millénaire, a new shopping centre, emerges above the flow of vehicles. This is a lively quarter, the cafés on the boulevard are welcoming, and the population, which is not uniformly white, seems to have properly taken possession. In short, for

once, 'it was not better before', when the Boulevard Macdonald was a desert crossing between the warehouses and
the Claude-Bernard hospital.

This hospital was very familiar to me from my work as
a surgeon. It stretched across a long strip of ground, from
the Porte d'Aubervilliers to the Canal Saint-Denis. Devoted
to the treatment of infectious diseases and tropical pathologies, parasitic and others, it dated from the early twentieth
century, when the idea of contagion was prevalent every-
where, so that it was made up of pavilions of a vaguely
colonial architecture, each a long way apart from the
others so that miasmas could not spread – to stop diphthe-
ria patients from catching malaria, or those with smallpox
catching sleeping sickness. Around 1970, a resuscitation
unit was established there, staffed by excellent doctors –
such as my friend Claude Gibert, whom I knew there as
my young senior registrar, capable of laughing at everything
while taking everything seriously, to the point of spending
his days and nights among the respirators, electric syringes
and monitors. In the unit where I worked, at the Laennec

New buildings on the Boulevard Macdonald.

© Cléo Marelli. Architect: Kengo Kuma & Associates

hospital, when a patient being operated upon was found to have an infection, we transported them to Claude-Bernard, where they would be better treated with no risk of contaminating the other patients. And I went there – we went there – almost every day to see how the case was developing and discuss the treatment with Gibert and others. Thirty or forty years later, these memories are both good and bad. Good, as the Claude-Bernard team was remarkable, with no swollen heads, no imposed morality, nothing of the subtly distilled contempt that doctors often exhibit towards surgeons. Bad, since often, despite all the care given, the infection won out, and to lose a patient in these conditions was particularly intolerable. My memory as a surgeon, in fact, contains more failures than successes, which is quite normal: simple consequences were by far the most frequent, and there is hardly any reason to remember those patients, whereas among the others there are some that remain as silent reproaches in a corner of my memory.

Returning west along the Boulevard Ney, this long segment of the Boulevards des Maréchaux was Jean Rolin's theme in *La Clôture*,[8] a book that gives in parallel the story of Maréchal Ney and a precise and often comic description of the boulevard that bears his name and the characters to be found there. At the start, there is the matter of the Bichat hospital:

If you stand with your back to the counter of the Au Maréchal Ney café, at the Porte Saint-Ouen, and look outward from Paris, you can see that the entire northeastern quarter of the crossroads is occupied by the Bichat-Claude-Bernard hospital, whose more modern and taller buildings are located on the edge of the Périphérique, and its older ones along the Boulevard Ney. On this side, the hospital wall, clad with bricks of a dirty yellow colour, and with openings that are scarce and protected by grilles, offers a forbidding spectacle.[9]

Among these openings, there is one, on the first floor, that was the window of the intern on surgical duty in the 1960s. As it overlooked the exit from the underpass of the Porte de Saint-Ouen, and given the intense night-time lorry traffic of that time (Les Halles!), there was no question of sleeping after night duty, when the inflow of patients finally calmed down.

In 1961, I was an intern here in the unit run by César Nardi. He was a good-looking man, an excellent surgeon, a *grand bourgeois* though not anti-Semitic, which was rather rare at that time and in that milieu. (When I decided to train as a surgeon, I was told that there was not a single Jew among the hospital surgeons of Paris. But this was not quite correct: José Aboulker, head of the neurosurgery unit at the Beaujon hospital, was not only a Jew but also a communist. His heroic role in the liberation of Algiers in 1942

Staff-room window of the Bichat hospital in the 1960s.

© Cléo Marelli

had brought him such prestige that the caste was forced to accept him.)

César Nardi was an enthusiastic golfer. One day when he was helping me with my first gastrectomy (which consists in removing all or part of the stomach), and having begun late we were still only at the preliminary stage, he said to me at the stroke of midday: 'Hazan, the Canada Cup has started, I have to leave you.' So I ended the operation with two young externs. In the post-operative care, I would go and see this patient three times a day, as it seemed to me so miraculous that I had completed the necessary procedure satisfactorily. This man, a local sculptor, was so grateful for this attention that after his discharge he presented me with his two favourite pieces, a deer's head and a bust of Beethoven.

We were then in the midst of the Algerian war, and the Bichat hospital often received patients with bullet wounds, sometimes from the police and sometimes from shoot-outs between FLN and MLA militants. In the unit, the sister in charge of the daytime team had the Algerian patients brought down to the basement the day before their operation, where the monitoring and care were extremely poor. When I was on duty, I had them taken back upstairs, so that one day Nardi asked me why I gave preference in his unit to North Africans. I asked him to accompany me to the basement, where he would not usually go, and he backed up my decision.

It is not easy to describe what a public hospital was like in a quarter such as Bichat in the early 1960s. In the afternoons, no doctor or qualified surgeon would be present, since they were all at their offices 'in town', or in their clinics. Admissions and operations were the responsibility of two interns, one medical and one surgical. For general anaesthetic you had to obtain telephone authorization from one of the two duty surgeons for the whole of Paris, who would be in the process of operating at Passy or Neuilly, and who always gave their blessing – in a friendly and casual manner – except in the case of a minor, when one of them had to be present, most often remaining in plain clothes at the door of the operating theatre. The outdated premises were more than full. In winter, at Bichat, black drapes were hung on the chapel walls and stretchers piled up there for the patients admitted at night – all pathologies and ages mixed together. No one found any cause to complain, they were all poor.

CHAPTER 8

I do not know of any other capital city where the transition from inside to outside is as marked as it is in Paris. In London, Tokyo or Berlin – not to speak of Cairo or Mexico City – it is none too clear where the boundary falls, and the very distinction between the city and its surroundings is vague. There are two main reasons, I believe, for the sharpness of the boundary in Paris. The first is the existence of the *portes*. In earlier times these had an evident material existence, when they were openings in the fortified wall. But even after the destruction of the *fortifs* in the 1920s, even without gates and officials, these are not places that you cross without being aware of it. They are dislocated spaces where you can expect to find the starting points of bus routes (with three digits instead of the two for those inside Paris), petrol stations and car washes, trams, signs indicating nearby destinations – Drancy, La Courneuve, Enghien – or distant ones, Melun or Lille. The original meaning of *porte* has not been eradicated.

The second element that makes the limits of Paris so clear-cut is the Boulevard Périphérique, far more so than the Boulevards des Maréchaux, which without the Périphérique would eventually have been digested, including their thin belt of social housing from the 1920s, built as the city continued its centrifugal growth. The Périphérique, with its wide footprint, its anti-noise barriers, its slip roads, and the new buildings that reinforce it with an almost uninterrupted strip of corporate ugliness, is something else again.

The Porte de Pantin at the turn of the century.

At the time of its construction, there were not many people who predicted that this road, mawkishly christened a 'boulevard', would constitute a terrible barrier between the old Paris and what might become the new. Louis Chevalier, one of the clearest minds of the time, describes a number of urban catastrophes in *L'Assassinat de Paris* – Maine-Montparnasse, the Italie quarter, La Défense, the massacre of Belleville, and of course Les Halles[1] – but if I am not mistaken, he has nothing to say about the Périphérique. Nor does Guy Debord mention it in *Panegyric*, published twenty years after its inauguration by the happily forgotten Pierre Messmer; according to Debord, 'this city was ravaged a little before all the others because its ever-renewed revolutions had so worried and shocked the world'.[2] The only person, I believe, who understood what was happening, was Jean-Luc Godard. In 1967, in *Two or Three Things That I Know About Her*, his description of the Paris in which Marina Vlady wanders – juke-boxes and pinball machines in the cafés, dark green cups with gold bands, Citroën Ami 6's and Peugeot 404's, *France-Soir* and the Vietnam war – is shown in a clashing counterpoint with shots of the works on the Périphérique, where the movements of cranes, concrete mixers and bulldozers are emphasized by sudden loud and almost painful sounds, bringing home the seriousness of the threat. The barrier imposed by the Périphérique is not only physical, it also affects the representation of the city. By confining Paris to the twenty arrondissements, it contributes to the image of a city that is mummified and museum-ified, in which working-class life is reduced to a more or less narrow sector, confined to the north-east between Montmartre and Charonne. But as this walk has confirmed to me, such an image is completely false. From Châtelet to the Porte de la Chapelle, in the heart of the historic city, the quarters I have crossed remain largely working-class. It is true that the pockets of gentrification are tending to expand, but this phenomenon still remains limited, even marginal. Whether in the Saint-Denis quarter, around the railway stations, along the faubourg and in the long valley of La Chapelle, the city I have walked through is a working-class one. Perhaps I more or less consciously chose my itinerary for this reason, and maybe my view would have been different had I started from the Rue Montmartre or the Rue du Faubourg-Poissonnière. But the fact that central and eastern Paris are largely working-class districts is not a recent phenomenon, as is well shown by the map of the barricades erected in the time of the June Days of 1848.

To classify quarters as 'working class' or not is a dichotomy that may fail to recognize the grey zones, encroachments, advances and retreats that shift from week to week. In the extreme case – the Rue des Francs-Bourgeois or the Rue de Verneuil on the one hand, the Rue d'Avron or the Avenue de Flandre on the other – the diagnosis is clear. But is the Place de la République, for example, working class? Yes and no. No, since almost all the cafés, shops and restaurants belong

The Barricades of February 1848

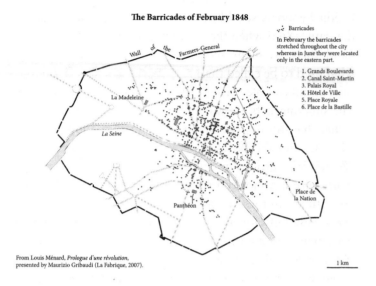

..·. Barricades

In February the barricades
stretched throughout the city
whereas in June they were located
only in the eastern part.

1. Grands Boulevards
2. Canal Saint-Martin
3. Palais Royal
4. Hôtel de Ville
5. Place Royale
6. Place de la Bastille

From Louis Ménard, *Prologue d'une révolution*,
presented by Maurizio Gribaudi (La Fabrique, 2007).

1 km

to chains, and what goes on there no longer has anything in common with the working-class life in which people meet their friends in such places or can chat with the owner. And yes, as the women and men who cross the square on foot, on bicycle or on a skateboard are a representative sample, varying according to the time of day, of the people of Paris. (Compared for example with the Place Saint-Germain-des-Près or the Place des Vosges, where, apart from tourists, the population represents a homogeneous and minority share of the human beings living in Paris.)

Despite all legitimate qualifications, there are certain markers to the working-class quarters. The Métro stations are dilapidated, the passages dirty, the escalators often broken and the exits equipped with anti-fraud systems that are unknown at La Muette or Franklin-Roosevelt. The police presence is constant and visible, showing that the object is to keep the poor quiet rather than to protect the rich. Bank branches are few and far between – just one, if I am not mistaken, along the long axis of La Chapelle, a

Crédit Lyonnais so old that you can still see on its façade the date '1863' when the bank was founded. On the other hand, there are many shops where you can send money to what used to be called the Third World. Others offer phone calls at unbeatable prices, or offer to 'unlock' your mobile. The supermarkets are 'super-discount', Leader Price or Dia rather than Monoprix. The cafés are Kabyl, the *tabacs* are Chinese, and the PMU betting shops always packed. On Wednesdays, groups of children set out on excursions, and whites are a minority in their multi-coloured ranks. And you can see in these quarters something that is for me the very symbol of sadness – an old Algerian worker alone on a bench with his imitation fur cap, his moustache and walking stick, or an elderly woman with swollen ankles, hobbling while she carries her shopping with difficulty in plastic bags.

The Boulevard Ney is so long that it borders on three adjacent communes – Saint-Denis in the centre, Saint-Ouen to the west and Aubervilliers to the east. To reach Saint-Denis,

Crédit Lyonnais façade, Rue Marx-Dormoy.

the end of this walk, several routes are therefore possible. You can follow the banks of the Canal Saint-Denis, in a dilapidated industrial landscape that crosses Aubervilliers, becoming residential when you pass into Saint-Denis, and even fashionable in the sector after the Pont du Landy: small white houses, clean surroundings, a well-kept landscape. Those living here are likely to be managers working close by in the newly built office blocks of the Plaine Saint-Denis.

Another possible path is to leave Paris by the Porte de Montmartre or the Porte de Clignancourt, cross the Foire aux Puces and then old Saint-Ouen obliquely towards the *mairie*. By avoiding major roads, this itinerary is full of charm, the streets are calm, bordered by low buildings with 'villas' here and there, cul-de-sacs in which each house has a garden. The Paris banlieue has dozens of quarters like this, from Clichy to Montreuil, Vanves to Gentilly. If the 'Grand Paris' project ceased to be a subject of political gestures, these pleasant enclaves could be taken as the starting point, instead of which they become islands in a sea of brutal ugliness.

After the *mairie*, you cross the Rue du Landy, a long transversal stretching from the Pont Saint-Ouen to Aubervilliers, whose name recalls that in the Middle Ages it was in these surroundings that the largest fair in the Île de France, the fair of Le Lendit, was held. A little further along is the Carrefour Pleyel, named in memory of Ignace Pleyel, a pianist and composer, pupil of Joseph Haydn, who founded a piano factory here in the early nineteenth century – both Chopin and Liszt used his instruments. Despite this noble origin, the crossroads has been dislocated by new constructions that seem thrown down at random – the central roundabout, moreover, is not round, and has no definable shape to respond vaguely to its surroundings. The ensemble is dominated by the Tour Pleyel. I belong to the probably rather small group of those who like this tower, its slight tapering, its rigorous metal curtain wall, its empty floor below the top and even the enormous and more or less elliptical advertising sign that rotates on top and at the moment vaunts the merits of Kia, the Korean car manufacturer. Today the metal is painted white, faded slightly grey by the weather, and is fine like that.

To reach Saint-Denis, I have chosen the simplest itinerary, the straight line along the A1 motorway starting from the Porte de la Chapelle. The first few metres are rough going, and only a few pedestrians chance to take the narrow path misguidedly named the 'Avenue de la Porte-de-la-Chapelle'. On the right is 'the bowling alley that occupies the ground floor of the multi-level car park wedged between the Périphérique, the motorway junction, the Boulevard Ney and the railway tracks cutting this diagonally', a passage from *La Clôture* that well evokes the crushing of walkers beneath a series of bridges between which the view of the sky and the open air are so narrow that they advance in a tunnel of concrete and metal.[3] To the left, I can see what used to be called the La Chapelle rubbish tip, now adorned with the sign CVAE (Centre de Valorisation et d'Apport des Encombrants): pyramids of debris, green lorries, black workers.

Once the last bridge is passed – the connecting slip road from the motorway to the westbound Périphérique – I continue parallel with the autoroute, covered after the first kilometre by a landscape improvement that was entrusted in the 1990s to Michel Corajoud, who also created the pleasant Jardin d'Éole that borders the Rue d'Aubervilliers. The plantations and street furniture manage to liven up a bit this endless straight line that bears the name Avenue du Président-Wilson, interspersed with car parks and ventilation shafts for the autoroute beneath. The gardeners have left room for vegetation, with a mixture of nettles

Concrete and metal tunnel,
Avenue de la Porte-de-la-Chapelle.

and weeds. In short, the worst has been avoided, which is certainly not easy. On both sides of this 'avenue' is a sad and dilapidated banlieue, with a multi-coloured but mainly black population.

All this suddenly changes once you cross the Rue du Landy. With the Stade de France, new office blocks housing the headquarters of big companies, SFR and SNCF, Bouygues and Matmut, a good part of the stock-exchange top forty installed in steel and tinted glass, this is the most striking architecture of the moment. The population are no longer the same, they are well dressed and you even hear English spoken. In the adjacent streets, instead of kebab shops and ruined warehouses, a line of luxury apartments stretches as far as the eye can see – an amazing transformation of the Plaine Saint-Denis which, after long having been the domain of heavy industry, was the very symbol of misery in this department only a short while ago. Be reassured, it has simply been pushed a bit further out.

At the end of the Avenue du Président-Wilson, the horizon suddenly widens. With the elevated curve of the A1 autoroute which turns eastward, the saucer on spikes of the Stade de France, the Canal Saint-Denis below forming a wide basin and the old town of Saint-Denis just close, this little hill creates a kind of frontier effect. To emphasize this, the apartment block that disfigures it should be pulled down and a monument erected in its place, for which Alexandre Vesnin or Erich Mendelsohn could be resurrected. This would emit invisible waves directed at the Tour Pleyel in one direction and the Saint-Denis basilica on the other, which has the only tower in the old town centre.

In reality, to get from Paris to Saint-Denis, almost everyone takes the Métro – line 13, the most neglected, the most irregular, always packed in its proletarian sector between Saint-Lazare and its northern destinations, Aubervilliers

Einsteinturm, Potsdam (Erich Mendelsohn 1917–1921).

and Gennevilliers. Emerging from the Basilique station, the quarter resembles the centre of Ivry, which is understandable as it was built by the same architect, Renée Gailhoustet. The result here is a little less convincing, even if we find the same raw concrete, acute angles, planted terraces and overhead passageways that give its Ivry counterpart its charm – most likely because this development is smaller and more dense, and the choice to build everything on stilts creates dark corners that are scarcely welcoming.

I had intended this walk to lead from one bookshop – Envie de Lire in Ivry – to another, and this other is here at the heart of this quarter, on the Place du Caquet. Folie d'Encre is both the opposite of and the equivalent to Envie de Lire. It is larger, lighter, more orderly, with no unstable piles or outside bins, but it is for Saint-Denis what Envie de Lire is for Ivry: a centre, a meeting point, a place of political animation. The owner, a woman whom we shall call S. and whose children come from East and West Africa, has been able to establish ties with the neighbouring cinema, the Gérard-Philipe theatre and even with the basilica, where she organizes lectures. Children come and do their homework among the books, voluntary organizations hold their meetings here, and the local people speak of 'their' bookshop. Gatherings for which mothers prepare African dishes take place not to discuss successful titles but rather questions facing a population who are in great majority Arab or black. 'Public hearings' are envisaged, which will not be debates where boredom is on the agenda.

The *mairie*, still communist today, supported the establishment of this bookshop in the town centre. On the Place Jean-Jaurès, its 'Third Republic' architecture sits next to the façade of the neighbouring basilica without too much discomfort. Nothing recalls the serious events that took place here between the wars, which is understandable since such disagreeable memories cannot help anyone. Yet it was Saint-Denis, and particularly its *mairie*, that saw the spectacular rise of Jacques Doriot: an engineering worker demobbed in 1918, leader of the Young Communists after the Tours congress, at the front of anti-militarist and anti-colonial struggle against the war in the Rif, deputy for Saint-Denis at the age of twenty-five when he came out of prison, and, as mayor of the town when he was thirty, the most popular member of the PCF leadership. But his opposition to the 'class against class' line would lead him first to a break with Thorez, followed by a drift into fascism that culminated in his alignment with the Nazis under the Occupation. A terrible story, of which I imagine many present-day inhabitants know nothing.

The Place Jean-Jaurès is the start of the Rue de la République, the town centre's pedestrian axis. It is reminiscent of the Rue du Faubourg-du-Temple, yet still more diverse if that is possible – veils, turbans, braids and dreadlocks, baseball caps, beanies – a whole world of young people, amid poor shops selling clothes and perfume, or unlocking mobile phones. The pace is slow and the ambience peaceful, as in an Oriental town. The most penetrating eye would not detect any symptom of embryonic gentrification, yet this is the very opposite of a ghetto, rather a different form of life that has taken root in this street bordered by working-class flats from the nineteenth century, where I feel as much at home as if I had always lived here.

It ends opposite a rather ugly church built by Viollet-le-Duc. Strange that this restorer of so many magnificent monuments – including the basilica at the other end of the street – should have been the author of such mediocre architecture when he turned to original work. Going round the church on the left, following the line of the RER and Transilien railways in a desolate landscape, you end up where the Canal Saint-Denis joins the Seine. A worn-out lawn and a few poplar trees mark the confluence. Let us hope this will remain as simple, and not undergo the fate of another meeting of waters, that of the Marne and the Seine spoiled by an ill-sited hotel in the form of a pagoda.

To return to Paris I walk through a landscape of shacks, recent buildings and construction sites until I reach the Saint-Denis station. Before arriving there, I learn from a hoarding, written in the style particular to this kind of announcement, that 'a new eco-quarter, a new way of living, an industrial heritage upgraded by the presence of artists, a quarter at the gates of Paris, connected, accessible and alive' is to be built here. In the overcrowded station, dirty and uncomfortable, you have to be careful not to upset the brutes of the Sécurité Ferroviaire and find yourself up against the wall, hands in the air, and intimately searched. The spectacle is permanent. Such are the two faces of Saint-Denis, one radiant, the other sordid and brutal, between the Californian 'Marlowe' of Raymond Chandler and the African 'Marlow' of Joseph Conrad.

Images of Paris have always been multiple and contrasting, from Baudelaire's 'Paris sombre' to the Hollywood dream of An American in Paris. And yet, at certain disturbing moments, when the city ceased to be 'a festival', a particular picture is constructed whose features are strangely similar in different epochs: a city threatened by the influx of foreign elements, by invasion – Paris was often taken as a metonym for France. Under the Second Empire, the guests of Princesse Mathilde – Taine, Flaubert, the Goncourt brothers – feared the Paris populace and were relieved by the crushing of the Commune, which according to Maxime du Camp was composed three-quarters of foreigners. Seventy years later, under the Occupation, Céline, Brasillach and Reba-tet denounced (sometimes in the literal sense) the Jews omnipresent in Paris, claiming that 'it took the insane dogma of equality between men for them to parade among us once more'.[4] Today, another seventy years on, ever more successful authors speak of 'Islamists' in the banlieues – especially in Paris – in the same way as Maurras treated the Jews and Dumas *fils* treated the rebellious workers. The same mixture of contempt and fear appears in their discourse, always with a police component, a more or less explicit appeal for a muscular response to those who trample on our precious 'values'. I am confident that Paris will shake itself up and get rid of this miasma once again. I would be tempted to follow the illustrious example of Stendhal, who wanted the words on his tomb to read: 'Arrigo Beyle, Milanese', since 'Parisian' is indeed what I feel myself to be, far more than French or Jewish – garments that do not suit me at all.

Having always lived in this great city of ten million human beings, I understand and am even sorry for those who live in the ghettos of the rich, and are scared when they emerge and see so many people who do not look like them. They reassure themselves by thinking that all will be well so long as they themselves, their newspapers and their TV channels, ensure the ever-lasting resignation of the Parisian people, of cashiers and waiters, bus drivers and building workers, unemployed, delivery drivers and illegal immigrants – this proletariat who people the streets I have crossed in this short walk across a much wider city. I think they are mistaken. I think that, with new music and words, this multi-coloured proletariat bears the inheritance of the memorable *journées* whose traces I have shown. Despite its disorganization, and its lack of clear awareness of this inheritance, it is united by the sense of its endless exploitation, and will show one day that the people have not lost the battle of Paris.

Notes

CHAPTER 1

1. Zone d'Aménagement Concerté, i.e., 'concerted improvement' – translator.

2. Ernst Jünger, *Journal de guerre*, Paris: Juilliard, 1990, p. 491.

3. Alexis de Tocqueville, *Recollections*, London: Macdonald, 1970, p. 136.

4. Victor Marouck, *Juin 1848* [1880], Paris: Spartacus, 1998, p. 101.

CHAPTER 2

1. J.-K. Huysmans, *Le Bièvre et Saint-Séverin*, Paris: Stock, 1898, p. 10.

2. Auguste Blanqui, *Maintenant il faut des armes*, Paris: La Fabrique, 2006, p. 397. This letter is dated 1 March 1879.

3. Laure Beaumont-Maillet, *Guide du Paris médiéval*, Paris: Hazan, 1997, p. 132.

4. To learn to date Paris buildings, see François Loyer's irreplaceable volume, *Paris XIXe siècle. L'immeuble et la rue*, Paris: La Fabrique, 1987.

5. The poem entitled 'Politique'. Written in 1831, it was published in 1853 in *Petits châteaux en Bohême*.

6. Louis Chevalier, *Les Parisiens*, Paris: Hachette, 1967, p. 360.

7. Gustave Lefrançais, *Souvenirs d'un révolutionnaire*, Paris: La Fabrique, 2012.

8. Georges Canguilhem, *Vie et mort de Jean Cavaillès* [1984], Paris: Allia, 2014.

CHAPTER 3

1. Léon Daudet, *Paris vécu*, in *Souvenirs et polémiques* [1929], Paris: Robert Laffont, 1992, p. 1073.

2. See on this subject Laure Lurat's excellent *Passage de l'Odéon*, Paris: Fayard, 2003.

3. Gustave Tridon, *Les Hébertistes*, Brussels, 1871, p. 38.

4. Dolf Oehler, *Le Spleen contre l'oubli. Juin 1848*, Paris: Payot, 1996, p. 22.

5. Francis Carco, *De Montmartre au Quartier Latin* [1927], Monaco: Sauret, 1993, p. 123.

6. Louis-Sébastien Mercier, 'Les Carrières', in *Tableau de Paris* [1781], Paris: 1990, p. 36.

7. See Jean-Pierre Babelon, *Demeures parisiennes sous Henri IV et Louis XIII*, Paris: Hazan, 1991.

8. Mercier, *Tableau de Paris*, p. 205.

9. Jean-François Cabestan, personal communication.

10. Gérard de Nerval, *Selected Writings*, London: Penguin, 1999, p. 220.

11. Louis Chevalier, *L'Assassinat de Paris*, Paris: Calmann-Lévy, 1977.

12. According to François Chaslin. Chaslin was a journalist at this time, and quotes an article of his from *Macadam* magazine in *Les Paris de François Mitterrand*, Paris: Gallimard, 1985.

13. See Françoise Fromonot, *La Campagne des Halles. Les nouveaux malheurs de Paris*, Paris: La Fabrique, 2005.

14. Mercier, *Tableau de Paris*.

15. Marcel Proust, *Time Regained. Remembrance of Things Past*, London: Penguin, 1983, vol. 3, p. 779.

CHAPTER 4

1. François Loyer, *Paris XIXe siècle*, Paris: Hazan, 1987.
2. On Meryon, in 'The Salon of 1859'. The whole passage runs:

   The majesty of accumulated stone, the bell-towers pointing their fingers to heaven, the obelisks of industry vomiting against the firmament their coalitions of smoke, the prodigious scaffoldings of monuments under repair, applying to the solid body of the architecture their modern architecture of such a paradoxical beauty, the tumultuous sky charged with anger and spite, the depth of perspectives augmented by the thought of all the dramas they contain, none of the complex elements of which the painful and glorious backdrop of civilization is composed was forgotten.

3. André Breton, *Arcanum 17*, Los Angeles: Green Integer, 2004, p. 159.
4. Marouck, *Juin 1848*, p. 37.
5. Charles Jeanne, À cinq heures nous serons tous morts!, introduced by Thomas Bouchet, Paris: Vendémiaire, 2011. See also Thomas Bouchet, *Le Roi et les barricades. Une histoire des 5 et 6 juin 1832*, Paris: Seli Arslan, 2000.
6. See Oehler, *Le Spleen contre l'oubli*.
7. *The Works of Heinrich Heine* (trans. Leland), vol. 7, London: Heinemann, 1893, 'French Affairs', p. 280.
8. Renzo Piano, *Carnet de travail*, Paris: Seuil, 1997.
9. See the excellent interview with Piano and Rogers by Antoine Picon in *Du plateau Beaubourg au Centre Pompidou*, Paris: Éditions du Centre Pompidou, 1987. The following quotations are taken from this work.
10. On all these points it is useful to read François Chaslin, *Un Corbusier*, Paris: Seuil, 2015.

CHAPTER 5

1. For further detail on these events, see Éric Hazan, *A History of the Barricade*, London: Verso, 2015, chapter 4.
2. Quoted in M. Vimont, *Histoire de la rue Saint-Denis de ses origines à nos jours* (3 vols), Paris: Les Presses modernes, 1936, vol. 1, p. 327.
3. Ibid., vol. 3, p. 51.
4. Ibid., p. 68.
5. Ibid., p. 83.
6. Ibid., vol. 2, p. 225.
7. Thierry Schaffauser, *Les Luttes des putes*, Paris: La Fabrique, 2014.
8. Walter Benjamin, *The Arcades Project*, Cambridge, MA: Harvard University Press, 1999, p. 42.
9. Daniel Stern, *Histoire de la révolution de 1848* [1850], Paris: Balland, 1985, pp. 619–20.
10. André Breton, *Nadja*, New York: Grove Press, 1960, p. 32. The printing works of *Le Matin* were on the corner of the Boulevard Poissonnière and the Rue du Faubourg-Poissonnière.
11. *Mémoires d'outre-tombe*, Book 32, Chapter 9.
12. Jean-Paul Sartre, *Words*, London: Penguin, 2000, p. 113.
13. Edmond and Jules de Goncourt, *Pages From the Goncourt Journal*, New York: NYRB Classics, 2007, p. 30.

CHAPTER 6

1. The specific character of the faubourgs is often lost in standard translations. Here for example, 'A squalid street shaken by heavy dump-carts' and 'In the muddy maze of some old neighbourhood' – translator.
2. Thomas Clerc, *Paris, musée du XXIe siècle. Le dixième arrondissement*, Paris: Gallimard, 2007, p. 13.

3. One of the sketches in *Paris vu par...* (1964). The others were the work of Jean-Luc Godard, Érich Rohmer, Claude Chabrol, Jean Douchet and Jean-Daniel Pollet.
4. A contemporary nickname for Louis Bonaparte – translator.
5. Excellent photos of these statues, with the names of their creators, can be found at: www.nella-buscot.com/jardins_paris_10_gare_du_nord_1.php.
6. Marcel Proust, *Within a Budding Grove. Remembrance of Things Past*, London: Penguin, 1983, vol. 1, p. 694.
7. On this painting, see Éric Hazan, *The Invention of Paris*, London: Verso, 2010, pp. 352–4.
8. Heroine of an eponymous comic strip – translator.
9. Anna Maria Ortese, *Silenzio a Milano*, Bari: Laterza, 1958. She is also the author of one of the finest books on Paris, *Le Murmure de Paris*, Paris: Mille et une nuits, 1999.

CHAPTER 7

1. For details, see Lucien Lambeau, *Histoire des communes annexées à Paris en 1859*, vol. 5, Paris: Ernest Leroux, 1923.
2. Victor Marouk, *Juin 1848* [1877], Paris: Spartacus, 1998.
3. Gérard de Nerval, *Selected Writings*, p. 207.
4. Maurice Culot (ed.), *La Goutte d'Or, faubourg de Paris*, Brussels: AAM, 1988.
5. Léon Gozlan, *Balzac en pantoufles*, Paris: Michel Lévy, 1862; cf. Hazan, *The Invention of Paris*, p. 324.
6. Marcel Proust, *The Captive. Remembrance of Things Past*, London: Penguin, 1983, vol. 3, pp. 1 and 113.
7. Sarah Kofman, *Rue Ordener, rue Labat*, Paris: Galilée, 1994; Robert Bober, *Quoi de neuf sur la guerre?*, Paris: POL, 1993.
8. Jean Rolin, *La Clôture*, Paris: POL, 2004.
9. Ibid., p. 23.

CHAPTER 8

1. Chevalier, *L'Assassinat de Paris*, part 3, 'Les pouvoirs et les choix'.

2. Guy Debord, *Panegyric, Volumes 1 and 2*, London: Verso, 2004, p. 38.

3. Rolin, *La Clôture*, p. 35.

4. Lucien Rebatet, *Les Décombres* [1942], in *Le Dossier Rebatet*, Paris: Robert Laffont, 2015, p. 138.

Index

À la Pinte du Nord, 130
À la Ville d'Aulnay, 130
À *Saint-Lazare,* Toulouse-Lautrec, 126
A1 motorway, 6, 171, 173
A3 motorway, 6
Abbaye, L', 25
Aboulker, José, 162
Age d'or, L' (Bunuel), 43
Aligre, 65
All the Boys are Named Patrick (film), 50
Altaroche, Agéno
'6 June! Mourning,' 85
An American in Paris (film), 176
Ancien Régime, 71
Anguier, Michel, 110–111
Anne of Austria, 41
Antoine, Jacques, 29
Antoine, Théâtre, 118
Anziutti, Jacques, 38
Apollinaire, Guillaume, 36
Apollo gallery, 61
Arab Goutte-d'Or, 137
Arago, François, 26
Arcanum 17 (Breton), 80
Archives d'Architecture du XXᵉ Siècle, 9
Arnault, Bernard, 63, 64
Arretche, Louis, 69
Assassinat de Paris, L' (Chevalier), 65–66, 166
Au Maréchal Ney, 160
Au Massif Central, 130
Au Train de Vie, 120
Aubervilliers commune, 169
Augé, Marc, 154

Augsburger Allgemeine (newspaper), 83
Auguste, Philippe, 55, 72
Autant-Lara, Claude, 1
Autrement Dit, 47
Avenue de Choisy, 8, 9, 10
Avenue de Flandre, 167
Avenue de la Porte-de-la-Chapelle, 171, 172
Avenue de la Porte-d'Ivry, 7
Avenue de l'Observatoire, 37, 38
Avenue Denfert-Rochereau, 31, 35
Avenue des Gobelins, 5, 16, 23
Avenue des Jeunes Filles Aveugles, 33
Avenue d'Italie, 5, 12
Avenue d'Ivry, 7, 8, 9
Avenue du Général-Michel-Bizot, 9
Avenue du Président-Wilson, 171, 173
Avenue Jean-Jaurès, 6
Avenue Kléber, 139
Avenue Maurice-Thorez, 6
Avenue René-Coty, 30
Avenue Simon-Bolivar, 9

Badinguet, 128
Bailly, Jean-Christopher, 47–48
'Bal des Ardents,' 23
Baltard, Victor, 96
Balto, Le, 46
Balustrade, La, 57, 120
Balzac, Honoré de, 33, 60, 99, 112, 113, 114, 145, 151
César Birotteau, 91

Comédie humaine, La, 35, 84, 112–113
Commission in Lunacy, The, 16, 113
Ferragus, 38–39, 112–113
Old Goriot, 41, 145
A Second Home, 75–76
A Start in Life, 97
Balzar, Le, 131
Barbès, 128, 141, 146, 147
Barrière de Montreuil, 143
Barrière d'Enfer, 27, 31
Barrière d'Italie, 13, 16, 139
Barthélemy, Joseph, 24
Bastille, La, 25, 99
Bastille, Théâtre de la, 130
Baudelaire, Charles, 55–56, 85, 113, 114, 116, 130, 133, 151, 176
Beach, Sylvia, 52
Beaubourg Centre, 91
Beaudoin, René, 60–61
Beaujon, 162
Beauvoir Hôtel, 39–40
Beaux-Arts, 44
Bédier, Joseph, 7
Benjamin, Walter, 30, 104
Berger, Patrick, 38
Bertrand, 43
Beverly, Le, 104
Bibliothèque de France, 158
Bibliothèque National de France, 23, 40, 102
Bicêtre, 72
Bichat hospital, 160–163
Bièvre, 17, 18, 23
Blanqui, Auguste, 11, 20, 92–93
L'Enfermé, 23
Blin, Roger, 131
Bloc des Gauches, 19
Blondel, François, 110, 117
'BNP Paribas,' 6
Bober, Robert, 153
Bofill, Ricardo, 69
Bofinger, 131
Bois de Boulogne, 64
Bolée, La, 59–60
Bonaparte, Louis, 101

Bonne Santé, La, 24
Bouffes-du-Nord, Théâtre des, 141
Bouillon Julien, 122, 131
Boulevard Arago, 18, 24
Boulevard Barbès, 145, 147
Boulevard Blanqui, 11, 18, 19, 20
Boulevard de Bonne-Nouvelle, 107, 110, 111
Boulevard de la Chapelle, 141, 145–146, 147, 148
Boulevard de la Villette, 110
Boulevard de l'Hôpital, 11, 15
Boulevard de Port-Royal, 39
Boulevard de Strasbourg, 111, 116, 118–119
Boulevard des Filles-du-Calvaire, 62
Boulevard des Italiens, 6
Boulevard des Maréchaux, 7
Boulevard d'Italie, 19
Boulevard du Temple, 78, 92
Boulevard Haussmann, 22, 79
Boulevard Kellermann, 17
Boulevard Macdonald, 157, 158, 159
Boulevard Magenta, 126, 127–128, 129, 147
Boulevard Malesherbes, 79
Boulevard Masséna, 7
Boulevard Montparnasse, 39, 43
Boulevard Mortier, 5
Boulevard Ney, 144, 157, 160, 169
Boulevard Périphérique, 165
Boulevard Port-Royal, 38
Boulevard Raspail, 33, 45, 139
Boulevard Saint-Denis, 101, 110
Boulevard Saint-Germain, 44–45, 53, 55
Boulevard Saint-Jacques, 30
Boulevard Saint-Martin, 78, 92, 110
Boulevard Saint-Michel, 31, 35, 39, 44–45, 47
Boulevard Sébastopol, 69, 77, 96, 100, 102, 106
Boulevard Sérurier, 22

Index

Boulevard Strasbourg, 77
Boulevards des Maréchaux, 139,
   160, 165
Bourse de Commerce, 69
Bourvil, 1
Brasillach, Robert, 176–177
Brassens, George, 59
Brasserie Flo, 124–125
Bréa, General, 12
Breton, André, 111, 112
   Arcanum 17, 80
   Mad Love, 80
   Nadja, 62
   'Vigilance,' 80
Bretonneau, 135
Brotherhood of Consolation, The
   (Balzac), 113
Bullet, Pierre, 110, 111, 117
Bunuel, Luis
   L'Age d'or, 43
Butte-aux-Cailles, La, 20
Buttes-Chaumont, Les, 127

Café Tournon, 52
Cahors, 37
Caillebotte, Gustave, 130
Calberson warehouses, 157
Calligrammes (Apollinaire), 36
Canal Saint-Denis, 158, 159, 170,
   173, 176
Canguilhem, Georges, 37
Cap 18, 156
Capra, Frank, 43
The Captive (Proust), 152
Carco, Francis, 59
Carpeaux, Jean-Baptiste, 40
Carrefour Pleyel, 170
Cartier, Fondation, 33
Catacombes, 28, 71–72
Cavaignac, Godefroy, 40
Cavaillès, Jean, 37
Céline, Louis-Ferdinand, 176–177
   Death on Credit, 99
Centre de Valorisation et d'Apport
   des Encombrants (CVAE),
   171
Centre Pompidou, 88
Centre Régionale d'Oeuvres

Universitaires et Scolaires
   (CROUS), 40
César Birotteau (Balzac), 91
Chambre des Notaires, 77
Chandler, Raymond, 176
'Chapelle highway, La,' 139
Chapelle International, 144
Chapelle-Saint- Denis, La,
   139–140, 145, 155
Charles VI, 23, 101, 106
Charles X, 84, 112
Charlus, 73
Chartier, 122
'Château of Queen Blanche,' 23
Chateaubriand, François-René,
   112, 113
   Mémoires, 83–84
Chateaubriand, Mme de, 32
Château-d'Eau, 78
Châtelet, 58, 72, 79, 167
Chausée-d'Antin, 78
Chénier, André, 107, 126
Chevalier, Louis, 27, 67–68, 166
   L'Assassinat de Paris, 65–66,
   166
Chez Jeannette, 123
Chez Papille, 31
Chez Paul, 62
Chez Tati, 148
China, 8
Chinatown, 138
Chirac, Jacques, 69
Chrestien, Charles
   Lost Illusions, 84, 107
Chronicle of a Summer (film), 42
Cieslewicz, Roman, 47–48
Cirque d'Hiver, 62, 117, 153
Citadines, 99
Cité Maurice-Thorez, 4
Clairvaux prison, 20
'Clara Clara' (sculpture), 10
Claude-Bernard, 158, 159–160
Clébert, Jean-Paul, 43–44
Clemenceau, Georges, 20
Clerc, Thomas, 116
Clichy, 26
Cloître Saint-Méry, Le, 85
Closerie des Lilas, La, 40

Clôture, La (Rolin), 160, 171
Cluny museum, 102
Cochin, 38
Cofinger, 131
Collége de France, 60, 67–68
Combray, 73
Comédie humaine, La (Balzac),
   35–36, 84, 112–113
Commission in Lunacy, The
   (Balzac), 16, 113
Compagnie, 48
Comptoir d'Escompte, 123
Comte de Provence, 51
Concert Layol, 122
Conrad, Joseph, 176
Conservatoire des Arts et Métiers,
   102, 104
convent of the Récollets (now
   Maison de l'Architecture), 117
Corajoud, Michel, 171
Cordeliers, 54
Corvisart Métro station, 20
Cosette, 15
Counterfeiters, The (Gide), 60
Coupole, La, 131
Cour Batave, 91, 94
Cour de Rohan, 55
Cour des Petites-Écuries, 124, 125
Cour du Commerce, 53, 55
Courbet, Gustave, 55–56
Courts of Miracles, 72
Crédit Lyonnais, 48, 169
CROUS (Centre Régionale
   d'Oeuvres Universitaires et
   Scolaires), 40
Culot, Maurice, 149
Cuvier, George, 5
CVAE (Centre de Valorisation et
   d'Apport des Encombrants),
   171

Dabit, Eugène, 116
Dalle des Olympiades, 8
Dalou, Jules, 10–11, 49
Danton, Georges, 54, 55
Danton café, 141
Darboy, Monsignor, 148
Daudet, Léon

Paris vécu, 50, 60
Davioud, Gabriel, 76–77
de Brosse, Salomon, 51–52
Death on Credit (Céline), 99
Debord, Guy, 166
Decerfz, Laure, 84
Découverte, La, 20
Dejean, 137
Delacroix, Eugène, 11, 49
Delahaye, 16
Delanoë, Bertrand, 87
Deneuve, Catherine, 69
Denfert-Rochereau, 27, 30
Dibbets, Jan, 26
Diligentes, 99
Divan, Le, 46
Doisneau, Robert, 20, 65
Doriot, Jacques, 175
d'Orléans, Philippe, 92
Dormoy, Marx, 142
Dubois, Antoine, 133
Duchamp, 47–48
Duchesse de Berry, 84
Duchesse de Longueville, 42
Dumas brothers, 177
Duras, Marguerite
   The Lover, 48
Dussoubs, Denis, 101
Duval, Jeanne, 133
Dynamic saloon, 7

Eastman, George, 9
Écluse, L', 59
École Coloniale, 35
École de Médicine, 54
École des Mines, 44, 47
École des Ponts et Chaussées, 29
École Normale Supérieure, 44,
   67–68
Écossaises, 99
Éditions de la Découverte, 20
Éditions de Minuit, 48, 58, 79
Éditions du Seuil, 55
Éditions Hazan, 47, 124
Éditions Maspero, 58
Einsteinturm (Potsdam), 173
Encelade, 21
Enfants-Bleus hospital, 97

Enfants-Rouge, 155
Enfants-Trouvés, 16
Enfermé, L' (Geffroy), 23
Envie de Lire, 2, 3, 174
Espace Expansion, 70
Estienne school, 20
Eugène, Louis, 40
Exposition Internationale, 9
'Eyes of the Poor, The'
    (Baudelaire), 114

Fabrique, La, 24, 105
Faculté de Droit, 117
Faubourg du Temple, 78
Faubourg Saint-Antoine, 78
Faubourg Saint-Germain, 79
Faubourg Saint-Marceau, 12, 16
Faubourg-Saint-Denis, 98
Favalelli, Max, 100–101
Fayard, 45
Félix Potin building, 100
Fénéon, Félix, 50
Férmiet, 40
Fernand-Widal, 133, 136
Ferragus (Balzac), 38–39, 112–113
Ferreri, Marco, 69
Figaro, Le (newspaper), 107–108
Filles de l'Union Chrétienne, 102
The Fire Within (Malle), 50
'5 and 6 June 1832' (poem), 85
Flammarion, 45
FLN, 24–25
Florentine Marie de Médicis,
    51–52
Folie d'Encre, 174
Fondation Eastman, 9
Fontaine aux Lions, 40
'Four Parts of the World,' 40
Foyot, 50
France-Soir (newspaper), 100
Françoise-Sagan, médiathèque,
    126

Gabin, Jean, 1
Gailhoustet, Renée, 3, 174
Gaîté-Lyrique, La, 102
Gallimard, Gaston, 58
Garaudy, Roger, 5

Gare d'Austerlitz, 141
Gare de l'Est, 6, 77, 111, 120,
    140, 156
Gare de Lyon, 130
Gare du Nord, 6, 117, 120, 127,
    128–129, 130, 131–133, 140,
    141
Gare du Nord (Jean Rouch
    segment in film *Paris vu par...*),
    120
Gare Montparnasse, 130
Gare Saint-Lazare, 129–130
Gare Saint-Lazare, La (painting
    by Manet), 130
Geffroy, Gustave, 23
Gehry, Frank, 64
George, Sylvain, 119
Georges-Pompidou, 136
Gérard-Philipe, 174
Giacometti, Alberto, 10
Gibert, Claude, 160
Gide, André
    The Counterfeiters, 60
Gittard, Daniel, 42
Godard, Jean-Luc, 166
    *All the Boys are Named
    Patrick,* 50
God's Rock, 119
Goldenberg, Jo, 137
Goncourt prize, 48
Goujon, Jean, 70–71
Goutte-d'Or, La, 140, 145, 146,
    147, 148, 149, 150
Grand Boulevards, 106
Grand Écran, 10
Grands Boulevards, 91–92
Grands Magasins Dufayel, 11
Grands Moulins de Pantin, 7
Grégoire, Mère, 16
Grémillon, Jean, 43
Guernica, 60
Guillaume Apollinaire, 8
Guillotin, Joseph-Ignace, 55
Guimard, Hector, 28

Hachette, 44–45
Halles, Les, 65–67, 68, 69, 70,
    87, 91

Hauranne, Duvergier de, 42
Haussmann, Georges-Eugène, 24,
  59, 75, 76, 77–78, 79
  Mémoires, 78
Hawks, Howard, 43
Hazan, 45
Heine, Heinrich, 83
Hennebique, François, 57
Henri IV, 61, 72
Henri Sauvage building, 153–154
Henry Brulard, 46
History of a Crime (Hugo), 101,
  109
Hôpital du Nord, 148
Hôtel de Beaufort, 92
Hôtel de Clisson, 56–57
Hôtel de Sens, 56–57
Hôtel de Ville, 75, 78
Hôtel du Lion d'Argent, 98
Hôtel Floridor, 30
Hôtel Hérouet, 56
Hôtel Lamoignon, 57
Hôtel Mercure, 6, 20
Hôtel Saint-Pol, 56
Hôtel-Dieu, 58–59
Huault, Gilbert, 34
Hugo, Victor, 16, 83
  History of a Crime, 101, 109
  Misérables, Les, 83
  Things Seen, 83, 108–109
Hulten, Pontus, 89
Humanité, L' (newspaper),
  107–108
Hune, La, 45–46
Huston, John, 43
Huysman, Joris-Karl, 17

Ibos, J.-M., 7
Île de la Cité, 59, 78
Île Saint-Louis, 79
Innocents, 70–71
Inspection Générale des Carrières
  de Paris, 28
Institut d'Art et d'Archéologie,
  35
Institut d'Astrophysique, 26
Institut de France, 61
Institut de Recherche et

Coordinational Acoustique/
  Musique (IRCAM), 86–87
Institut des Cultures d'Islam, 149
Institut des Sourds-Muets, 46
IRCAM (Institut de Recherche et
  Coordinational Acoustique/
  Musique), 86–87
Italie Deux, 10
Ivry, 2, 3, 4, 174

Jacques London (print works),
  37
Jardin d'Éole, 171
Jardin des Plantes, 5, 18, 43
Jeanne, Charles, 81
Jeanne d'Arc, 143
Jewish quarter, 137
Joie de Lire, La, 45, 57–58
joli Mai, Le (Marker), 42
Jolie, Angelina, 122
Jourdain, Frantz, 63
Journal de Guerre (Jünger), 10
Joyce, James, 52–53
Julien, 122
June Days of 1848, 11, 13, 26,
  52, 140, 148, 167
Jünger, Ernst, 10

Kengo Kuma agency, 158
Kodak, 9–10
Kofman, Sarah, 153
Koons, Jeff, 89

Labrouste, Henri, 134
Labrouste, Théodore, 134
Laennec hospital, 30–31
Lajarrige, Bernard, 35–36
Lapin Agile, 59
Lariboisière, Comtesse, 148
Lariboisière hospital, 128
Larousse, 45
L'Assommoir (Zola), 147–152
Latin Quarter, 12, 26, 42, 44, 45,
  59–60
Law, John, 92
Lazareff, Pierre, 100, 101
Le Balto, 46
Le Balzar, 131

le Bel, Philippe, 71
Léautaud, Paul, 60
Ledoux, Claude-Nicolas, 11–12,
　25, 28
Lefrançais, Gustave
　Souvenirs d'un révolutionnaire,
　29–30
Left Bank, 12, 42, 43, 44, 45, 46,
　53, 55–56, 57, 139
Leibniz, 52
Lemercier, Valérie, 41
Lendit, 170
Lenin, Vladimir, 36
Léo Malet, 8
Libéral Bruant, 15
Libération-Sud movement, 37
library of the Prince de
　Guermantes, 72–73
'ligne de Sceaux,' 39
Ligue des Droits de l'Homme,
　28–29, 106
Lindon, Jérôme, 48, 58
Lion de Belfort, 27, 30–31
'Little Old Women, The'
　(Baudelaire), 113
London, Jacques, 37
Lost Illusions (Chrestien), 84,
　107
Louis XIII, 61
Louis XIV, 93, 106, 110–111
Louis XVI, 51, 92, 99
Louis XVIII, 51–52
Louis-le-Grand, 35
Louis-Philippe, 84
Louvre, 61, 75, 106
Louvre-Lens, 63
Louxor, 146
The Lover (Duras), 48
Loyer, François, 77
Lubitsch, Ernst, 43
Luchini, Fabrice, 122
Lucien Leuwen (Stendhal), 82–83
Luxembourg, 21–22, 39
Luxembourg garden, 49
Luxembourg palace, 51–52
LVMH, 64
Lycée Fénelon, 55
Lycée Louis-le-Grand, 4–5

Lycée Montaigne, 35, 40
Lycée Turgot, 25

Mac-Mahon, 43
Mad Love (Breton), 80
Madelonnettes, Les, 25
Maeght, Aimé, 36
Mairie-d'Ivry station, 3
Maison de l'Architecture, 117
Maison des Amis des Livres, La,
　52
Maison Dorée, 6
Maison Dubois, 133–135
Mallarmé, Stéphane, 130
Malle, Louis
　The Fire Within, 50
Manet, Édouard, 130
Mans, Le, 7
Mansart, Jules Hardouin, 41
Marais, 56
Marat, Jean-Paul, 54, 55
Marie-Lannelongue, 9
Marie-Thérèse, 32
Marker, Chris
　Le joli Mai, 42
Marne, 176
Martineau, Henri, 46
Maspero, François, 45, 58
Mastroianni, Marcello, 46, 69
Mathilde, Princesse, 176
Matin, 111
Maurras, Charles, 177
Maxime du Camp, 176
Médicis fountain, 40
Melville, Jean-Pierre, 65
Mémoires (Chateaubriand),
　83–84
Mémoires (Haussmann), 78
Mémoires d'outre-tombe, 32–33
Mendelsohn, Erich, 173
Mercier, Louis-Sébastien, 46, 61,
　71
Métro, 139
Mevlana bookstore, 122
Michel, Louise, 126
Millénaire, Le, 159
Minotaure (magazine), 36
Minuit, 45

Misérables, Les (Hugo), 83
MK2 Parnasse, 42
Mobilier National, 21, 22–23
Moi, un noir (film), 42
Mona Lisait, 60–61
Monde, Le (newspaper), 107–108
Mondor, Henri, 15
Monet, Claude, 23, 130
Moniteur, Le, 45
Monnaie, 29, 61
Monner, Adrienne, 52
Montagne Sainte-Geneviève, 12, 16, 44
Montmartre, 40, 127
Montparnasse, 42
Moreau, Hégésippe '5 and 6 June 1832,' 85
Moreau, Jean-Charles, 22
'Morning Twilight' (Baudelaire), 114
Muet, Pierre le, 41
Murger, Henri, 134
Mutualité, 19

Nadja (Breton), 62
Nardi, César, 162
Nathan, 45
Necker, 65
N'entre pas sans violence dans la nuit (film), 119
Nerval, Gérard de, 25–26, 111, 134, 145
  October Nights, 64–65
  Odellete, 49–50
New Morning, 125
Ney, Maréchal, 40, 160
Noailles, Marie-Laure de, 43
Notre-Dame, 59, 78, 128
Notre-Dame-de-Lorette, 104–105
Notre-Dame-des-Victories, 99
Nouvel, Jean, 6, 10, 33

Observatoire, 26, 31, 34–35, 39
October Nights (Nerval), 64–65, 145
Odellete (Nerval), 49–50
Odéon, Théâtre de l', 50, 51
Oehler, Dolf, 57

Oeuvre des Jeunes Filles Aveugles, 33
Office for Metropolitan Architecture (OMA), 158
Old Colombe, 149
Old Goriot (Balzac), 41, 145
Opéra, 127
Ortese, Anna Maria, 133

Pajou, Augustin, 72
Palace, Hôtel, 30
Palais de Justice, 58–59, 61, 62, 76–77
Palazzo Pitti, 51
Palazzo Publico, 88
Panegyric (Debord), 166
Panhard & Levassor, 7–8
Panthéon, 12
Parc de Choisy, 22
Paris cemetery, 3
Paris insolite, 44
Paris Métro, 69
Paris vécu (Daudet), 50, 60
Parnasse, 42
Parthenon, 35
Pascal, 19
Passage Basfout, 97
Passage Brady, 118
Passage de la Trinité, 97
Passage de l'Industrie, 118
Passage du Caire, 103, 104
Passage du Désir, 117
Passage du Grand-Cerf, 92–93, 97, 99
Passage du Marché, 116
Passage du Ponceau, 102
Passage du Pont-aux-Biches, 106–107
Passage du Prado, 121–122
Passage du Thermomètre, 22
Passage Saint-Foy, 102
Paulownias, 10
Peintaparis, 78
Perce, George, 119
Père-Lachaise, 11, 148
Périphérique, 5, 6, 45, 144, 158, 159, 165–167
Perrault, Claude, 34–35, 41

Perre, Auguste, 22–23, 143
Petit Pot Saint-Denis, Le, 111
Petite-Roquette, La, 26
Petit-Pont, 58–59
Philharmonie, 6, 10
Philippe VI de Valois, 23
Piano, Renzo, 86–87
Piano and Rogers Building, 87–88
Picasso, Pablo, 60
Pilon, Germain, 71
Place d'Alexandrie, 104
Place Dauphine, 61, 62
Place de France, 61–62
Place de Grève, 25
Place de la Chapelle, 127, 136,
  139, 141–142
Place de la Concorde, 117
Place de la Nation, 10
Place de la République, 10–11, 78,
  79, 128, 167–168
Place de la Sorbonne, 41, 45
Place de l'Assomoir, 149
Place de l'Odéon, 45–46
Place Denfert-Rochereau, 27, 31
Place des Innocents, 94
Place des Petits-Pères, 99
Place des Victoires, 99
Place des Vosges, 168
Place d'Italie, 5, 10, 11, 15, 17
Place du Caire, 103, 104
Place du Caquet, 174
Place du Châtelet, 75, 76–77
Place du Docteur-Yersin, 7
Place du Panthéon, 44
Place Gambetta, 41
Place Hébert, 156
Place Jean-Ferrat, 6
Place Jean-Jaurès, 174, 175
Place Napoléon-III, 128
Place Royale, 61, 62
Place Saint-André-des-Arts, 57
Place Saint-Germain-des-Près, 25,
  41, 45–46, 168
Place Saint-Michel, 31, 57, 59
Place Saint-Sulpice, 42, 45
Plaine Saint-Denis, 170, 173
Plekhanov, Georgi, 36
Pleyel, Ignace, 170

Poisson, Jeanne, 107
Polytechnique, 44
Pompidou, Georges, 66, 67–68
Pont d'Austerlitz, 18
Pont de Tolbiac, 8
Pont Mirabeau, 8
Pont Saint-Michel, 31
Pont-Neuf, 59, 61, 62–63
Porte d'Aubervilliers, 157, 158
Porte de Bagnolet, 22
Porte de Clignancourt, 170
Porte de la Chapelle, 6, 144, 157,
  167, 171
Porte de la Villette, 158
Porte de Montmartre, 170
Porte de Pantin, 6, 166
Porte de Saint-Ouen, 161
Porte des Lilas, 5
Porte des Poissonniers, 145
Porte d'Ivry, 5, 6
Porte du Grand-Châtelet, 71
Porte Maillot, 154
Porte Saint-Denis, 97, 107, 108,
  110, 111, 116, 120–121, 127
Porte-Saint-Martin, Théâtre de l',
  110, 111
Port-Royal, 37–38
Portzamparc module, 158
Potin, Félix, 100
Poussin, Nicolas, 20
Rebecca, 61
Préfecture de Police, 58–59
Pré-Saint-Gervais, Le, 22
Presses Universitaires de France,
  45
Proust, Marcel, 79, 152
  The Captive, 152
  Time Regained, 72, 73
Prouvé, Jean, 87
Pucheu, Pierre, 24–25

Quai des Grands-Augustin, 59
Quai d'Orléans, 79
Quai Malaquais, 44
Quatre-Fleuves fountain, 40
Quoi de neuf sur la guerre?
  (Bober), 153

Racine, 122
'Rag-Pickers' Wine, The'
    (Baudelaire), 116
Raspail, François-Vincent, 29, 42
Ravaillac, François, 72
Rebatet, Lucien, 176–177
Rebecca (Poussin), 61
Rem Koolhaas, 158
Renaissance, Théâtre du, 111
Renaudie, Jean, 3
Renoir, Jean, 43
République, 127
RER B, 30
RER station, 69
Réveil du 10e, Le, 116
Revolution, 55
Rey-Dussueil, Marius, 85
Richelieu, Cardinal, 42
Right Bank, 9, 43, 44, 45, 56, 87,
    127
Robert Laffont, 45
Robespierre, Maximilien, 55
Rochefoucauld, La, 39
Rochelle, La, 25
Rolin, Jean, 160, 171
Rol-Tanguy, Henri, 28
Rond-Point, Théâtre du, 117
Rosenberg, Léonce, 36
Roth, Joseph, 52
Rouch, Jean, 42, 120
Rouquet, Le, 123
Route de Fontainebleau, 12
Rude, François, 40
Rue Abel-Hovelacque, 20
Rue Affre, 148
Rue Aubry-le-Boucher, 81
Rue aux Fers, 71
Rue Beauregard, 107
Rue Bénard, 30
Rue Berger, 70
Rue Bernard-Palissy, 79
Rue Blondel, 110
Rue Boissonnade, 34
Rue Bonaparte, 45, 46
Rue Casimir-Delavigne, 51
Rue Cassini, 34–35, 35–36, 37,
    124
Rue Charlemagne, 52

Rue Chénier, 106
Rue Cléry, 107
Rue Corvisart, 20
Rue Crébillion, 51
Rue Croulebarbe, 16, 21, 22–23
Rue d'Aboukir, 106
Rue d'Alexandrie, 103
Rue d'Alsace, 120, 121, 140
Rue d'Arcole, 58–59
Rue d'Assas, 39, 40
Rue d'Aubervilliers, 140, 156,
    157, 171
Rue Dauphine, 60, 61
Rue d'Avron, 143, 167
Rue de Bac, 43
Rue de Belleville, 5
Rue de Bièvre, 19, 43
Rue de Caire, 103, 104
Rue de Champ-de-l'Alouette, 16
Rue de Chartres, 149
Rue de Choisy-le- Roi, 116
Rue de Cléry, 106, 107
Rue de Clignancourt, 11
Rue de Condé, 50, 51
Rue de Courcelles, 79
Rue de Dunkerque, 127
Rue de Faubourg-du-Temple, 5
Rue de Faubourg-Poissonnière, 5
Rue de Jessaint, 145
Rue de Jeûneurs, 107
Rue de la Chanverie, 83
Rue de la Chapelle, 6, 140, 142
Rue de la Charbonnière, 149
Rue de la Chaussée-d'Antin, 22
Rue de la Clef, 25
Rue de la Contrescarpe, 16, 43–44
Rue de la Ferronnerie, 72
Rue de la Glacière, 18
Rue de la Goutte-d'Or, 149
Rue de la Grange-Batelière, 37
Rue de la Harpe, 31
Rue de la Huchette, 31, 57–58
Rue de la Lune, 106, 107
Rue de la Montagne-Sainte-
    Geneviève, 43
Rue de la République, 175
Rue de La Reynie, 72
Rue de la Roquette, 130

Rue de la Santé, 24–25
Rue de la Verriere, 80–81
Rue de l'Abbé-de-l'Epée, 46, 47
Rue de Lappe, 130
Rue de l'Échiquier, 122, 123
Rue de l'École-de-Médicine, 53, 56
Rue de l'Évangile, 156
Rue de l'Hirondelle, 59
Rue de l'Odéon, 51, 52
Rue de l'Ouest, 49
Rue de Maubeuge, 127
Rue de Ménilmontant, 116
Rue de Montlhéry, 116
Rue de Nesle, 60
Rue de Palestro, 97, 100
Rue de Panama, 152
Rue de Paradis, 125
Rue de Paris in Les Lilas, 5–6
Rue de Rennes, 79
Rue de Rivoli, 77
Rue de Seine, 44, 45
Rue de Sévigné, 29–30
Rue de Sofia, 146
Rue de Suez, 152
Rue de Tolbiac, 8, 9
Rue de Tournon, 50, 51, 52
Rue de Tracy, 102
Rue de Venise, 91
Rue de Verneuil, 167
Rue de Vert-Bois, 79
Rue Dejean, 153
Rue d'Enfer, 27, 31–32
Rue d'Enghien, 122, 124
Rue des Amiraux, 153
Rue des Archives, 56–57
Rue des Arcis, 80–81
Rue des Boucheries, 53
Rue des Cordeliers, 22
Rue des Degrés, 106
Rue des Deux-Gares, 120
Rue des Francs-Bourgeois, 56–57, 167
Rue des Gardes, 149–150
Rue des Grands-Augustins, 60
Rue des Innocents, 70
Rue des Islettes, 149
Rue des Italiens, 107–108

Rue des Lions-Saint-Paul, 56
Rue des Lombards, 72
Rue des Marmousets, 24
Rue des Poissonniers, 5, 147, 149, 153, 154
Rue des Prêtres-Saint-Séverin, 31
Rue des Pyramides, 143
Rue des Pyrénées, 9
Rue des Quatre-Fils, 56
Rue des Rosiers, 137
Rue des Saints-Pères, 29
Rue des Ursulines, 42, 46
Rue d'Hauteville, 123
Rue d'Olive, 155, 156
Rue Doudeauville, 145, 152
Rue Drouot, 22
Rue du Calvaire-de- l'Évangile, 156
Rue du Château-d'Eau, 116, 118
Rue du Croissant, 107, 108
Rue du Faubourg-du-Temple, 175
Rue du Faubourg-Poissonnière, 123, 147
Rue du Faubourg-Saint- Martin, 116, 117
Rue du Faubourg-Saint-Denis, 116, 122, 123, 124, 125, 126–127, 129, 133, 136, 139
Rue du Faubourg-Saint-Jacques, 26, 36–37
Rue du Figuier, 56–57
Rue du Four, 79
Rue du Général-Lasalle, 105
Rue du Jardinet, 55–56
Rue du Landy, 170, 172
Rue du Moulin-des-Près, 20
Rue du Pont-de-Lodi, 60
Rue du Puits-de-l'Ermite, 25
Rue du Roule, 62–64
Rue du Sabot, 79
Rue du Temple, 56
Rue du Tourniquet-Saint-Jean, 75–76
Rue du Val-de-Grâce, 41
Rue du Vert-Bois, 107
Rue du Vieux-Colombier, 42, 79
Rue Dussoubs, 101

Rue Étienne-Marcel, 96
Rue Ferdinand-Duval, 137
Rue Frédéric-Sauton, 43
Rue Gabriel-Péri, 2
Rue Gayette, 120
Rue Grénéta, 92–93, 95
Rue Guénégaud, 45, 46
Rue Gustave-Geffroy, 23
Rue Gustave-Goublier, 118
Rue Guynemer, 49
Rue Hamelin, 79
Rue Hautefeuille, 55–56
Rue Henri-Barbusse, 31, 38
Rue Hittorff, 117
Rue Jacob, 45
Rue Jean-Dolent, 24
Rue Jeanne-d'Arc, 143
Rue Jules-Chaplain, 42
Rue La Fayette, 102, 117, 127
Rue Labat, 153
Rue Laffitte, 104–105
Rue Mahler, 25
Rue Maître-Albert, 43
Rue Marie-Stuart, 99
Rue Marx-Dormoy, 140, 142, 169
Rue Maubuée, 81
Rue Mauconseil, 92–93
Rue Mazarine, 46
Rue Méchain, 36–37
Rue Meslay, 79, 106
Rue Messier, 25
Rue Monsieur-le-Prince, 45, 51
Rue Montorgueil, 99, 100
Rue Mouffetard, 16, 43–44
Rue Myrha, 145, 152
Rue Nationale, 7
Rue Notre-Dame-de-Nazareth, 79, 106–107
Rue Notre-Dame-de-Recouvrance, 107
Rue Notre-Dame-des-Champs, 39
Rue Ordener, 143, 145, 153
Rue Ordener, rue Labat (Kofman), 153
Rue Pajol, 155
Rue Pavée, 56–57
Rue Philippe-de-Girard, 140
Rue Pierre-Bullet, 117

Rue Pierre-Sarrazin, 56
Rue Planche-Milbray, 80–81
Rue Poissonnière, 107
Rue Polonceau, 149, 150
Rue Popincourt, 138
Rue Quincampoix, 92
Rue Racine, 31, 45
Rue Rambuteau, 92, 96
Rue Réamur, 96, 100, 101
Rue Rébeval, 105
Rue René-Boulanger, 111
Rue Riquet, 143
Rue Royer-Collard, 47
Rue Saint-André-des-Arts, 53, 59
Rue Saint-Antoine, 25
Rue Saint-Denis, 70, 71, 72, 77, 92, 93, 94, 95, 96, 97, 99, 100, 101, 102–103, 104, 106
Rue Sainte-Croix-de-la-Bretonnerie, 56
Rue Saint-Honoré, 69, 143
Rue Saint-Jacques, 27, 31, 35, 42, 46
Rue Saint-Lazare, 99
Rue Saint-Martin, 77, 80–81, 83, 88, 91, 99, 106
Rue Saint-Maur, 148
Rue Saint-Merri, 81, 84, 85–86
Rue Saint-Paul, 56
Rue Saint-Séverin, 45, 57–58
Rue Saint-Sulpice, 51, 52
Rue Sedaine, 138
Rue Serpente, 55–56
Rue Sorbier, 22
Rue Stephenson, 141, 149
Rue Tholozé, 43
Rue Transonian, 95
Rue Turbigo, 25, 79, 96
Rue Vavin, 154
Rue Vergniaud, 18
Rue Victor-Cousin, 42
Rue Vieille-du-Temple, 56
Rues Gît-le-Coeur, 60

Sacré-Coeur, 104–105
Saint Phalle, Niki de, 40, 86
Saint Séverin, 58
Saint-Bernard church, 148

Index

Saint-Denis, 6, 95
Saint-Denis basilica, 173
Saint-Denis commune, 169, 171,
    173, 174–176
Saint-Denis-de-la-Chapelle church,
    143
Sainte-Geneviève, 134
Sainte-Jeanne d'Arc basilica, 143
Sainte-Pélagie, 25
Saint-Esprit Cosmétique, 119
Saint-Eustache, 64, 69
Saint-Germain-l'Auxerrois, 61
Saint-Gervais, 52, 61
Saint-Jacques-de-la Boucherie,
    79–80
Saint-Jacques-du-Haut-Pas,
    41–42, 46, 61
Saint-Joseph church, 148
Saint-Laurent church, 117
Saint-Lazare, 125–126
Saint-Leu church, 92–93, 96
Saint-Loubert Bié, Jérôme, 24
Saint-Martin-des-Champs, 104
Saint-Médard, 16
Saint-Michel fountain, 57
Saint-Nicolas-des-Champs, 81,
    111
Saint-Ouen commune, 169
Saint-Paul, 52, 71
Saint-Quentin, 128
Saint-Simon, 93
Saint-Sulpice, 42
Saint-Victor abbey, 18–19
Saint-Vincent-de-Paul, 33, 117,
    123, 125–126
Salpêtrière, 15
Samaritaine department store,
    62–64
Sand, George, 84
Santé, La, 24–25
Sauvage, Henri, 63, 154
Sauval, Henri, 71
Say sugar refinery, 16
Schaffauer, Thierry, 101
Schiffrin, Jacques, 36
Second Empire, 78
Second Republic, 26
A Second Home (Balzac), 75–76

Secrétan, 155
Sections Spéciales, 24–25
Seine, 4, 43, 45, 59, 176
Seine-Saint-Denis, 59
Serra, Richard, 10
Seuil, Le, 45
'Seven Old Men, The'
    (Baudelaire), 116
Seyrig, Delphine, 131
Shakespeare and Company, 52–53
Silenzio a Milano (Ortese), 133
'6 June! Mourning' (poem), 85
Snégaroff, Thomas, 36–37
Société des Amis de la
    Constitution, 54
Société des Amis des Droits de
    l'Homme et du Citoyen, 54
Société des Missions Évangéliques,
    26
Société des Saisons, 95
SOHO (Small Office, Home
    Office), 144
Sommier, 118
Sorbonne, 44, 102
Soufflot, Jacques-Germain, 117
Souvenirs d'égotisme, Les, 46
Souvenirs d'un révolutionnaire
    (Lefrançais), 29–30
Species of Spaces (Perec), 119
Splendid, Le, 116
Square de Choisy, 9
Square de l'Abbé-Migne, 30
Square du Chapeau-Rouge, 22
Square Émile-Chautemps, 102
Square Louvois, 40, 102
Square Montholon, 102
Square Paul-Painlevé, 102
Square René-Le Gall, 18, 20–21,
    22
Square Séverine, 22
Stade de France, 172, 173
A Start in Life (Balzac), 97
Stendhal (Marie-Henri Beyle), 19,
    177
    Lucien Leuwen, 82–83
Stern, Daniel, 109–110
Stohrer, 99
The Story of My Life, 84

Strasbourg-Saint-Denis, 91–92, 106, 110
Stravinsky fountain, 86
Studio 28, 43
Studio Bertrand, 43
Sudac, 16
'Sun' (poem), 151
Surrealists, 36

Tailhade, Laurent, 50
Tange, Kenzo, 10
Tartine du Nord, La, 130
Temple, Carreau du, 155
Terminus Nord, Le, 130–131
TGV de l'Est, 120
Things Seen (Hugo), 83, 108–109
Third Republic, 9, 28, 55, 62, 102, 174
Thorez, Maurice, 4, 5
Time Regained (Proust), 72, 73
Tinguely, Jean, 40, 86
Tocqueville, Alexis de, 13
Touche pas la femme blanche, 69–70
Tour de Nesle, 60, 71
Tour Montparnasse, 130
Tour Pleyel, 170–171, 173
Tour Saint-Jacques, 79–80
Trarieux, Ludovic, 28–29
Tribunal de Commerce, 58, 77, 119
Tridon, Gustave, 54–55
Trip Across Paris, The (film), 1, 36
'Triumph of the Repulic,' 10–11
Two or Three Things That I Know About Her (film), 166–167

Uccello, Paolo, 61
Ulysses (Joyce), 52–53
Unibail, 70
Union (print works), 36–37
The Unknown Masterpiece, 60

Val-de-Grâce, 38, 41–42
Valjean, Jean, 15
Vasconi, Claude, 69
Velasquez, Diego, 21–22
Vesnin, Alexandre, 173
Vian, Boris, 149
Vierge de douleur (Pilon), 71
Vigiere, D'Astier de la, 37
'Vigilance' (Breton), 80
Vigo, Jean, 43
Villa Medici gardens, 21
Ville, Théâtre de la, 76
Villejuif, 3
Villette, La, 40
Villon, François, 65
Viollet-le-Duc, Eugène, 175
Visconti, 40
Vitart, M., 7
Voisambert, 80–81
Vuitton, Fondation, 64

Wall of the Farmers-General, 5, 10, 11, 27, 115, 139, 143
Weiss, Michel, 9
Wittgenstein, Ludwig, 70

ZAC Bédier, 7
Zola, Émile, 147–148, 149, 150–151